Cover watercolor by
Sally McNamara,
with permission.

St. Thomas at St. John's, 1972

Scoring the Winning Touchdown, SJU 14 - CST 10

The Player's Tale

Life lessons from St. John's University,
Collegeville
1969 - 1973
William McNamara

Second Edition

Copyright 2006 and 2008 by William McNamara

All rights reserved. No part of this book may be
reproduced in any form, except for the inclusion of brief
quotations in reviews, without permission
in writing from the author.

Published and printed in the USA
by InstantPublisher.com

ISBN 978-1-60458-347-2

1 2 3 4

Dedication

This book is dedicated to my daughters
Kate, Gwen, and Mary.
You grew up way too fast.

Table of Contents

Foreword - Second Edition	13
Foreword - First Edition	15
The Last Blocking Dummy	21
Panty Raid	25
Education	29
Bennies: For Better, For Worse, Forever	33
Roommates	36
Godawful Summer Job	41
Two-a-Days	45
The Johnnie-Tommie Conundrum	49
Dorms	53
Another Side of Gagliardi	57

Drink	61
Road Trip	65
The Johnnie Football Adage	69
Living the Nightmare	73
Missed Dreams	77
Benedictine Bad Boys	81
Injuries	85
Sex and the Lonesome Johnnie	89
Zen and the Art of Blocking	93
Good Deeds	97
Winning in Perspective	101
To Reno in a Torino	105
A Lesson from Sports	109
Be Here Now	113
More than a Game	117
Drugs	121
Religion	125
War	129
Great Plays	133
Farewell	137

New Stories

Discrimination	141
As Only Freshman Are	145
Money	149
A Life Less Frantic	153
A Great Game	157
Values	161
Classic Moments	165

Foreword - Second Edition

      Writing the first version of this book was done in a bit of a fog. I knew the basic anecdotal yarns I wanted to tell, but there was always the feeling that some stories were missing. Since the first publication came out, a number of new tales have come to mind. Some are from the requests of others and some are from my own memories. I believe the added seven stories round out my experiences at St. John's.

      I also was quite naive about my writing skills in the push to finish the first edition. The intervening two years have helped me clean up the text. It's not perfect, but it's coming along.

Foreword - First Edition

When I am comfortable in the easy chair watching television, I wonder if I did all that I could have done to prepare my children for their journey through life. Life lessons are those moments where we learn about our relationship to the world and how to conduct ourselves so to get along. They tend to not be dramatic moments; rather, they usually pass without much notice. One has to be observant to recognize and learn from these everyday events that shape our existence.

In my youth, my father stressed that a person had to learn his or her own life lessons for him or herself, alone. Without much guidance, I experienced some of life lessons over and over again before I figured them out. But my father's and my youth were from a different time. Life was less hectic then; people and events moved slower, no instant communication, more freedom to learn from mistakes, not so much materialism and less social pressure.

Today it is hard to forge ahead on your own without help. You cannot confer life lessons to others, but you can be understanding and help guide. Children will learn their own life lessons in spite of overbearing and good intentioned parents. I wrote this book with that ideal in mind. I hope this book will give some direction to those on that journey when they feel lost and discouraged.

This book contains many of my life lessons as I remember them. I learned them during my college years at St. John's University in Collegeville, Minnesota. St. John's is a Catholic, liberal arts, all men's college founded in 1856 with an abbey and preparatory school run by the Benedictine religious order. The student body size is about 2,000 and there is a Germanic culture present from the original mission of serving the newly arrived German immigrants that settled the area.

The approximately 2,400-acre campus established then has changed little over the years, which has given rise to the phrase, "Pine Curtain." As with Winston Churchill's "Iron Curtain," the Pine Curtain has the effect of blunting the encroachment of the outside world. In that pastoral setting, the campus is a place of serenity and seclusion.

I came to St. John's in the fall of 1969 as an immature youth and left in the winter of 1973 as a somewhat mature adult. Many of the life lessons I learned at St. John's were not immediately evident to me until years later, but the seeds were planted. It took time for the comprehension to sink in.

When my nephew Kevin started playing football at St. John's as I had done thirty plus years earlier, the life lessons I had learned then started to come back to me. With children no longer in tow when attending football games, I could wander about without constantly looking for food and bathrooms. St. John's is a great place to reminisce; it doesn't change much so one is easily transported back in time. I would leave a game at half time to walk about, lose track of time and return late in the second half. Warm fall Saturday afternoons are a great way to experience St. John's.

I had the good fortune of having played football at St. John's while John Gagliardi was coach. Many of my life lessons revolved around football and John. I know that if I had not gone to St. John's, I still would have learned my life lessons, they just would not have been as unique. Once, when I was in a class John was teaching, he took out a letter a past player had just written to him. The letter was full of thanks for giving direction to that writer's life. John was bewildered. He didn't see himself as someone who helps develop people's lives. He saw himself as a football coach. Well, I agree with that writer. Whether he likes it or not, John was a powerful teacher and role model to many people on and off the field.

My time at St. John's was a brief moment, just four and one-half years. Life then was different than today, as today will be different from tomorrow. Everything changes so cherish the day; tomorrow will take it away.

The Player's Tale

The Last Blocking Dummy

It is difficult to separate the person from the myth when talking about a legend. John Gagliardi and his St. John's football program fit into that category. One piece of folklore that developed at St. John's was the legend of no blocking dummies used in practice. Blocking dummies are 75-pound canvas duffel bags, four feet high and stuffed with cotton. They have straps on them for holding onto by one person as another "blocks" it.

It was the first practice of two-a-day sessions my freshman year in 1969. A horde of a 100 or so players had trekked over the hill and were on the practice field running the first drill of the season, hitting blocking dummies. Yes, as I live and breathe, Johnnie football players were hitting blocking dummies.

Every lineman knows the drill; the first one in line holds the dummy, the next one up blocks it for five yards, then the blocker becomes the dummy holder, the holder goes to the end of the line and the next player up blocks. Up and down the practice field the dummy is pushed as the line of players snakes around.

Over the years I had learned the trick of dummy blocking—don't hit it low. A low hit drives the dummy into the ground, creating friction with the ground and that makes the blocker expend more energy to move it. If the blocker hits high and keeps pushing up, the dummy is driven back, getting the standard five yards of blocking distance and the blocker saves energy for the next drill.

On my turn, I hit the blocking dummy high and surprised the holder, who lost his balance and started falling backwards. The holder made a quick side step, trying to shake me off so he wouldn't fall down and he pulled the dummy with him. As the dummy was pulled to the side, I rolled my body in order to keep contact with the dummy so I would not land in the dirt. The end result had me pushing the dummy while on my back looking up, almost sitting on the dummy.

Suddenly there was a whistle and I heard John discussing my technique as everything you should not do when blocking. "You don't sit on your opponent. You apply the shoulder pad." My thinking was that sitting on the opponent would have kept the opponent out of the play, but that didn't sound very intelligent so I kept quiet. I was thoroughly raked over and chastised. I thought my career was over on the first day of practice. As soon as John finished with me, we started a new drill. That afternoon at practice, the blocking dummies were gone. The dummies did not appear for the rest of the season and during the next four years they never materialized again.

Did that incident start the Johnnie vanquished blocking dummies tradition? Later that year I was vindicated on my technique. That was when during a game, one of the offensive linemen performed the same maneuver. He executed a perfect pass block, driving the defensive lineman to the outside, behind the quarterback and out of the play. The defensive lineman fell down and the blocker stayed with him by sitting on him as the play continued. The opposition had a gang tackle going on our quarterback. They were driving him back and heading for those two players. Our offensive lineman got up at the last second and walked away just as seven or so bodies fell on the downed lineman.

It was a classic Monday night game film moment. One John ran back and forth with the team roaring in laughter. The difficult roll and sit block had finally gained respect.

Panty Raid

As a high school football player, I dreaded the homecoming dance. It was the girl thing. There was the ritual of trying to find a girl to ask to the dance who wouldn't say no, getting the only suit you had cleaned and trying to not look the fool for one evening. Why ruin a perfectly good game with that frivolous embellishment!

During my freshman year in college, I was happy to have nothing to do with homecoming except football. As the campus geared up for the homecoming, I quietly went about my own business. On a hot and humid evening during homecoming week, as I was outside for some fresh air, a crowd of students came running by yelling "Panty Raid!" They offered to take me along so I jumped into a passing car. As we drove by the library I spotted a fellow football player, Tom, walking along and minding his own business. As we drove by we stopped suddenly, grabbed Tom and dragged him into the back seat of the car. Then off we drove to an unknown adventure.

Now you would expect that a person thinking about becoming a priest would not swear but Tom let us have it for forcing him to come along on this immoral excursion. Nevertheless, by the time we got to St. Benedict's, the all girls' school associated with St. John's, he was game to see what this activity was all about. The car parked about four blocks from the college and we joined about fifty or so other Johnnies quietly running through the school grounds. When we were outside a dorm, the lads started yelling, "Panty raid! Panty raid!"

Tom and I brought up the rear, not quit sure about what we were doing and making sure there was a clear path in the opposite direction if needed. We watched in amazement as a rain of women's underwear and dainties were thrown from the dorm windows. One fell close to me. It was as small a brassiere as one can be. One step up from a T-shirt, I held it up like a trophy walleye.

Suddenly the dorm's double doors crashed open and out ran a nun in flowing black robes, shaking her fists in the air. She was yelling something about protecting the innocence of her charges and for us to go away. Tom and I, having both gone to Catholic grade and high school, knew full well what to do—run and run fast. We started running and didn't stop until we got back to the cars. We would have run the full four miles back to campus but most of the other Catholic educated students had already arrived and were driving off in great haste. We jumped into the first car we could and never looked back.

I have learned over the years that avoiding angry nuns is the best course of action. It saves the knuckles from ruler hits and other embarrassments. Some of the students, who must have gone to public schools, didn't understand the gravity of the situation and attempted to be confrontational. Big mistake. She would not back down. She kept running toward the raiders, looking as menacing as could be. Eventually the big strong men broke and ran, leaving their manhood in disgrace.

That was the last panty raid that I participated in. In my sophomore year, I actually had a date and I went to the homecoming dance. There was a panty raid that year also, but I didn't go. Again it had been a bit ugly and confrontational. The dance that year was held in Waite Park, a small suburb of St. Cloud, at an old dance hall. Sometime after that dance the hall burnt down. Don't mess with nuns!

Little did I know then that my homecoming dance experiences had come to an end after my sophomore year. The next two years I was injured in each homecoming game and did not make it to the dance. I had asked the same woman to all three dances, but after going one out of three, she dumped me. Same old girl thing.

Education

After graduating from St. John's, I have consistently heard from others that they felt St. John's graduates were well schooled and educated. I initially considered my years there to be no different than they would have been at any other school. But, with the passage of time, I came to understand what they meant.

A St. John's education is the total package, as much the classroom experience as the environment. A college professor is a college professor, some are good and some are bad. I had all types at St. John's. The monks were in the position of not teaching for money or advancement, but to educate. You felt their kinship to the reverence of learning, you were not just trying to complete a class. And of course, the minimal amount of activities on campus would drive many students to study, just to do something.

In those days, St. John's had a 4-1-4 system. Four months of regular classroom study, one month of "January Term," followed by another four months of regular classroom study. The January terms were required for graduation, but there was no credit given. You could design your own course, like reading books and writing a report or traveling the world. My January Terms defined my education more than the classroom experience did.

One year I took a class called "Love and Sex in Cinema." Watch a movie in the morning, eat lunch, take a nap and then watch a second movie in the afternoon. To a college student, that was heaven on earth. In addition, the cinemas slowly progressed from philosophical love, to sexual love, to pornography. Of course, in a tasteful, academic way! That made the wind-swept tundra a bit more bearable that winter.

Another year I went to British Columbia, Canada, for missionary work with a group called the Frontier Apostolate. The highlight was riding in a train with a sleeper berth for two days each way, just like in a 1930's movie. I ended up at a town next to an Indian reservation called Fort St. James where the only store in town, the Hudson Bay Company, still bartered in animal pelts. It was at the end of civilization. Dirt roads out of town generally went nowhere.

Another January Term had me as an orderly at the St. Cloud Hospital, in the geriatrics ward. I was quickly cured of ever wanting to get into the medical field.

I learned a lot about teaching and learning from a teacher who taught an Educational Psychology class. He started the first class by setting down the rules. You didn't have to come to class except for the last day when you wrote down your name and the grade you wanted. He was telling the students that he wanted us to come to class to learn, not take up space. I went to every one of his classes, probably from a guilt complex. He wasn't the greatest of teachers, but I admired his ideals. He knew that education is what you make of it. If you didn't want to work, don't waste the time.

Another unique teacher was in Psychology, which I considered as dull as a course could be. To get the class stimulated, he took out a handgun and shot a blank into the ceiling, then asked the class to write about what they had just experienced. I suspect he would be fired in today's world, but it started me thinking outside the box. I learned that there are more ways to look at a situation than what you first contemplated.

While taking a calculus test with a pen, the professor, who was a monk, came up to me and said offhandedly. "Taking a math test with a pen, huh! Well then, you are either awfully goddamn smart or awfully goddamn stupid." I remember that profound statement when judging others who are doing something in a way that I wouldn't.

As the years progressed, the classroom became more and more dear. Every class period was anticipated, every minute was an opportunity to learn. The more you learn the more you want to learn. The quest for knowledge perpetuates itself.

Then a day comes and it's all over. Suddenly it's graduation time and that which was your lifeblood is now a poison. Everyone you know is leaving and you can't stand to be on campus. You are forced to take the next step, to go out into the real world with your educational experiences as your guide.

Bennies: For Better, For Worse, Forever

The women at the College of St. Benedict were the lifeblood of the men of St. John's. They also were the butt of many a joke, but a lot of Johnnies ended up marrying Bennies. It's funny how people tend to mistreat the ones they love.

My first experience with Bennies was at the Freshman Welcome Dance in the fall of 1969 at the old St. John's gym, Rat Hall. It was a big event for me. The dance actually had a live band. In high school, a dance was where everyone stood around the gym listening to records classmates brought from home. Rat Hall was spiffed up, as much as an old building can be. Johnnie freshmen were milling around outside as the buses came and dropped off the Bennie freshmen.

Almost immediately wise guys were calling out numbers from one to ten, rating the women as they stepped off the bus. Creative insults included telling a few to get back on the bus. One hopeful Johnnie was asking the women if they wanted to have sex with him. It was a very low percentage proposition, but when asked about that, he stated he only needed one to say yes. Somehow, through the animosity, everyone got into the gym and the dance started.

There are two types of people at dances, the movers and the wallflowers. The movers get dancing right away and keep it up all night. The wallflowers just look out over the floor and keep standing at the wall as the evening wears on. I was with the wallflowers, men on one side and women on the other. When the dance is about over, the male wallflowers get forlorn and make a desperate move to ask some woman, any woman, to dance. The rush was on to get at least one dance in for the price of admission.

I was one of the lucky ones, I got a dance in. Being a nerd in high school, I had already learned the drill—always ask the pretty girls to dance. Maybe it's because the pretty ones take pity on nerds, but they tend to dance with you where the less than pretty girls get satisfaction from blowing you off.

I never really understood why the Johnnies gave the Bennies such a hard time. There was a homecoming talent show at St. Benedict's and the Johnnie student newspaper ran a caricature of it, showing cows walking on a promenade in a beauty contest.

Many a Friday night my freshman year was spent sitting in Mary Commons student center at St. Benedict's, watching and trying to meet women while talking to other Johnnies who were watching and trying to meet women. I would go to parties at St. Benedict's, but I would end up never talking to anybody. About the closest relationship I had with a Bennie was riding on the same bus seat.

After that first semester, I pretty much avoided St. Benedict's, there is only so much groveling one can do. Over the years, however, my appreciation for Bennies manifested itself. It was the little things they did. When I was in the hospital, I received cards and food sent by Bennies. That's what the Bennies were all about, they were there when you needed them.

As the years progressed, the Bennies became more like sisters to the Johnnies. St. Benedict's can be as quiet and lonely as St. John's. You learn to appreciate people for who they are, especially over the long, cold winters. We needed each other. By my senior year of school, it was amazing to see how many quality relationships had developed.

Now, when I see a graduate of St. Benedict's, a smile crosses my face. I have developed respect for them over time, they proved their mettle from behind the Pine Curtain. They are the professional businesswomen that hold their own against men, the educated women that show their acumen and the soccer moms who see beyond the carting of kids back and forth.

It was not just the quality of education at St. Benedict's, but the integrity that was developed. The Bennies had the last laugh over the Johnnies.

Roommates

In college, men and women receive two educations. One is book learning through classes and the other is interpersonal relationship development through roommates. Roommates can be heaven, hell, or somewhere in-between.

My first roommate was from a small, central Minnesota town. The college matched us up before we arrived. We both were tall, involved in athletics, science majors and could have been twins for all the similarities between us. We never connected. I don't even remember if we ate many meals together.

We had run against each other at a high school track meet and he had beaten me. I remembered during the meet that between races, he was leading a group of fellow teammates in homework, using the chalkboard on the field to write down calculus equations. My high school didn't teach calculus so I was impressed.

His most apt quotation was "Don't trust anyone in a suit." I didn't think much about it then, but now I see that he was ahead of his time. He left at the end of the school year and I went looking for a new roommate.

My second roommate and I found each other when we were the last two people on the floor to not have a roommate for the next year—not a good beginning. He was from out west and he was very smart. We were cordial enough to each other, but again, I don't remember if we ever ate much together.

One memorable event that year was being awakened in the middle of the night to him being violently sick. He had found my jug of homemade wine and he had helped himself to a fair amount of it. It was a rough night and I have not favored wine since.

In the early spring of my sophomore year, knowing I was a loner, I had an epiphany. I had better start looking for roommates early to find compatible ones or I would suffer the same fate as in past years. I got lucky and landed two excellent roommates, Steve and Tom, with whom I played football. Tom was a bit scary; he was about my size and could be a wild man, but very gentle inside. Steve was the quiet, studious type. We didn't hang on each other, but we did eat many meals together.

That spring semester, Steve and Tom decided to take an exchange semester at a sister college, which was located out of state. There was a shortage of dorm space so I was asked to take in a new roommate. I had collapsed my lung in football the previous fall and I could not tolerate cigarette smoke. I advised my new roommate about that and he agreed to not smoke in the room. The next day I walked into the room and found a teepee in the middle, with smoke billowing out of the top. He said it was ok because the teepee was a different room. He was gone the next day.

I immediately got another new roommate who had just returned from the Vietnam War. He wore his army fatigues and army boots all the time. He was thinking of joining the seminary, but I suspect the seminary didn't want him. He would sit and stare out into space for hours, not talking. He was a bit too strange. I discussed it with the Dean and he agreed. That roommate was moved out and I was spared any further roommate roulette. Steve and Tom were back for our senior year and we had a superb time.

Now this tale would generally have ended there but since I was coming back as a fifth-year senior to play football, I still had more roommates to live with. That summer I joined five Johnnie graduates at our first place away from school, a two-bedroom apartment in the Twin Cities. It ended up being an animal house. We had no beds, just mattresses on the floor, a sofa and TV, clothes piled high in the corners and a few chairs with a table. The sink could not hold another dirty dish. The shower leaked and with excessive use, the foundation of the building sunk. We were all gone within four months. The landlord agreed to refund the damage deposit if we would just leave. To this day, you can still see the patched bricks on one end of the building where it was repaired.

That fifth-year senior semester I lived in St. Cloud with students from St. Cloud State at a boarding house. I was up at 6:30 A.M. to student-teach, went to football practice and returned home by 7:00 P.M. to prepare the next day's lessons. This place was also an animal house. I tired of the mess so I started washing all the dirty dishes in the sink each night when I got back, just to have a clean plate for supper and because I didn't want to live in a zoo any more. My housemates would ask me why I did it and I would answer, "Because." They were trying desperately to avoid all responsibilities and I was doing what I thought was right for the house and for me.

I graduated in December and moved out. I returned in the spring to visit the house and I noticed that the sink was always cleaned up. Developing quality interpersonal relationships can have a positive effect; it got them to clean up after themselves.

Godawful Summer Job

Some of the best practical advice I received from John Gagliardi was this, "Take the most godawful summer job so that you can't wait to get back to school in the fall." By either chance or happenstance, I was the poster child for that maxim.

My first godawful summer job experience was during the summer after my senior year of high school. I had visited St. John's and John found out that I would not turn eighteen until school started in the fall. I was underage for most summer jobs so he had a fellow football player give me a job lead, to work on a railroad track gang in St. Paul.

I went down to the rail yard as innocent as one can be. As I walked over the train tracks and around the huge freight cars, a slow moving boxcar just about ran me over. I was scared out of my mind. As I interviewed for the job, inside a small shack with the biggest group of miscreants you ever saw, I gave my real age instead of lying as I had been told. "Sorry son, you gotta be eighteen to work here," growled the foreman. Those were the sweetest words I have ever heard. The Johnnie who gave me the job tip grabbed my shoulder and chided me for not giving an older age as he had told me to do, but it was the best truth I had ever spoken. I ran like hell from that place.

Later that summer I worked a job sweeping out Metropolitan Stadium in Bloomington after Twins baseball games. We were picked up a van at the Bethel Hotel, a place that worked with homeless men. My buddy said it was a good job and that we would get paid in cash every night.

We caught the last two innings of the game and then we sat and waited as the stadium cleared out. Then everyone took a section and swept it out with a broom, from top to bottom, one section after another, until about five in the morning. Most of my fellow workers managed to find a lot of left over beer and an occasional, mostly empty, bottle of hard liquor. The van ride back was like being in a police drunk tank. When it was time to go to school that fall, I was already packed.

The next summer was spent at a steel pre-fabrication manufacturing plant, working with heavy steel. I had such tasks as stacking one-inch steel plates while standing behind a hydraulic shear, grinding off burrs on freshly cut I-beams with an air chisel, working on mocked-up bridge beams drilling rivet holes ten feet off the ground, flipping newly painted steel beams and cutting angle iron with a press just inches from my fingers. It was a constant series of smashed fingers, bumped shins and broken down old men talking about their lost dreams.

It was the graveyard shift and many of the workers would come in dead tired from their day jobs or occasionally drunk. When I worked in the bridge bay, drilling rivet holes ten feet off the ground, even though it required two men on the drill, I would have my partner sleep it off and I would do the drilling by myself. It was safer.

It was a good job, paid well, but the workweek started at midnight on Sunday night. How I dreaded Sunday evenings, having to get ready for work when others were getting ready for bed or were still partying. When Friday morning came, the weekend started for me. I would have to wait for my friends to finish their jobs so that by the afternoon I would be dog-tired and would end up going to bed. I loathed that job. I counted off every hour of every day, waiting for school to start. When it was time to head for St. John's and start two-a-day practices, I was ready. I could now sleep nights. I worked that job for three summers, pretty much guaranteeing that I would finish college.

I must admit that I did break that rule one summer after I had injured my lung playing football. I had a bad wheeze that would not go away. By good fortune I ended up going to Nevada that summer, working at Lake Tahoe. The hot and dry air there cleared up my lungs, much better than Minnesota's humidity would have. This time I did lie about my age (I was under 21) and got a job working in a casino. The problem with a great summer job is that you don't want to leave. The bohemian lifestyle was grand, great weather and lots of debauchery. I was torn between returning to St. John's and staying. But common sense took over. Living in a tourist town is not healthy. No one changes. The workers eventually move on or burn out.

At the Reno Airport, as I drifted in and out of blissful memories of the past summer, I heard the stand-by seating attendant calling out some very odd pronunciations of "McNamara." After the third twisted attempt I stood up and yelled "Here." Taking the last seat on the plane, I was off to school. What a waste it would have been if I had not gotten on that plane.

Two-a-Days

Every year since 1965, when I was a high school freshman, in mid-August I'd get a knot in my stomach. That's the time of year when two-a-day practices for football start. The body had learned by the angle of the sun, by the hot and humid dog days of summer that it is time for the suffering of two-a-days. By Labor Day when school starts and even the most barbaric coach can no longer have two-a-days, the foreboding is over.

I was a gasper. I never seemed to get enough air when I was involved in strenuous activity as a youth. Today I would be diagnosed with athletic asthma, but in the 1960s, you just sucked it up and pushed yourself. Gulping in air with one knee on the ground or hunched over with both hands on my knees was my typical football stance.

My first association with two-a-days was at Hill High School, a Catholic high school in St. Paul. As unbelievable as it sounds, the core coaches then were ex-St. John's players: Bob Sullivan, who eventually became the head coach at Carleton College; Bob Stolz, an All-American who had the best adage for an offensive lineman, "If you forget who to block, just hit somebody!"; and Roger Ludwig, who John would use as an exemplar every year by showing an old game film in which he made the first seven or so tackles in a game.

But somehow they all missed the lesson from Gagliardi on easy practices; they ran a two-a-day session from hell. One drill I still have nightmares over was called the Burma Road, from World War II fame. Five blocking dummies were lined up in two parallel lines about ten yards apart. You pumped your feet and took off running to tackle the first dummy. After tackling the dummy you jumped up, reversed direction, pumped your feet, run to the next dummy and tackled it. Back and forth, zigzagging until you hit all ten dummies. Your legs felt like rubber and ached so badly you could hardly walk. Then you lined up to do all it again. How we stayed conscious is a mystery to me.

The high school two-a-day practices were the most painful times in my life that I have ever endured. To get through a two-hour session, I would tell myself that I would quit as soon as the practice was over. Of course, I always came back for the next session. No matter how discouraged I get with a problem today, I just remember back to those high school two-a-days. I now know that I can endure anything.

If not for the Vietnam War, I may never have played collegiate football. Football was my only way into college and to stay out of the draft. As a high school senior, football was low on my short list of goals. Two-a-days and I had an acrimonious relationship. So in mid-August 1969, when that sinking feeling overtook me, I found myself up at St. John's for two-a-days. Little did I know what was waiting for me.

I discovered that St. John's did not have a rough and tough workout regiment for two-a-days or regular practices. Instead, the practices were notoriously easy and that aspect was even boasted about. I do not know how it goes today, but back then the practices were enjoyable. It takes an extraordinary coach with tremendous faith in his players and his program to not be tempted to drill hard to prove the players' mettle. There are very few coaches like John.

Yet even at St. John's, on occasion, I would be gasping for air. Practice consisted of the endless running of play after play after play, for an hour at the same spot. In a game, we either moved up the field and scored a touchdown or we lost possession. We were never on the field for more than five to ten minutes at a time.

My one and only football coaching job was as a seventh-grade coach at Cold Spring, Minnesota, in 1978. I was asked to help out with a seventh-grade team and the fellow who had run the team previously was more than willing to let the new blood take over. I ran it strictly Gagliardian, after spending the first practice showing the players how to put on their equipment. We did only one or two drills at practice. No endurance training, no synchronized drills, no yelling your lungs out, no blocking dummies and no blocking sleds. We ran play after play after play. They went undefeated and un-scored upon until the last game of the season. The Gagliardi system works.

A trained athlete can mentally force their body to play on when the flesh is screaming to stop. Pain becomes easy to manage when you are in a resolute state of mind. Pride plays hard. Coaches need to understand that and to believe in their players. Let the players save their game for Saturdays.

The Johnnie-Tommie Conundrum

The first thing all St. John's football players and students learn at school is the "Beat St. Thomas" mantra. In the 1960s as it is today, the College of St. Thomas was the nemesis of St. John's. They were the other Catholic, all-men's liberal arts college in Minnesota. The distinctions between the two are that St. Thomas is an urban school, located in St. Paul, Minnesota, and has a distinctive Irish bent. St. John's has an obvious rural setting and a strong German inclination. St. Thomas has since gone co-ed and is now known as the University of St. Thomas.

Beating St. Thomas makes the season, in any sport, no matter what the record. A loss to St. Thomas is embarrassing and if you were otherwise undefeated, death. The reciprocal is also true—you can lose every game in the season but if you beat St. Thomas, it wasn't such a bad season. Especially if you knocked St. Thomas out of contention. I know it's the same at St. Thomas.

It wasn't until track season in the spring of my freshman year when I actually met a Tommie in person that I learned they didn't always drool and actually could speak in full sentences. As the old joke goes:

Two men are in the bathroom and one says to the other, "You must be a Johnnie!"

"How did you know?"

"By the dribble down the front of your pants."

"And you must be a Tommie!" the Johnnie observes.

"How did you know that?"

"I saw your class ring when you were picking your nose."

One year, St. Thomas was up in St. Cloud playing the Huskies in football. A number of Johnnie football players went over to watch the game. We were cheering for St. Thomas to win. As St. Cloud was driving for the go-ahead touchdown in the last minute of the game, the Tommie defense forced a fumble on the goal line to win the game in dramatic fashion. That was a strange feeling, cheering for St. Thomas. We walked away with our heads spinning. Can't make a habit of that.

A Tommie at a steel prefabrication company gave me my first real summer job. The company was a big booster for the University of Minnesota Gopher hockey program and a number of the university student-athletes worked there. As I was being given the "Don't call us, we'll call you" routine, the personnel manager noticed that I was a Johnnie and mentioned that he was a Tommie. I fibbed a little by stating that the St. Thomas football team had been good that year. The next day, he called and gave me a job. It was on the graveyard shift and not on the second shift or day shift with the university hockey players. I did notice the large class ring on his finger.

That scenario repeated itself a few summers later. While living with five other Johnnies, I met with the personnel manager at the Hamm's Brewery for a summer job. At the interview, we had discussed our respective colleges and he mention he was a Tommie. Again, I stretched the truth about how good the Tommie football team had been that year. He later called and offered me a job. I had just started working at another company but he gave my roommates jobs, but of course, on the graveyard shift. He also had a large class ring on his finger. In those days, breaks in the brewery included drinking free beer at the in-house bar. Talk about Johnnies in hog heaven.

After college I have made numerous Tommie friends. One in particular is an attorney, Charlie. We figured out that we had been lined up opposite each other and had actually knocked heads many years earlier.

Without a doubt, my greatest Johnnie/Tommie connection occurred when I married a Tommie—please, a woman, Stephanie. My future wife was attending the co-ed graduate school at St. Thomas at the time. We were both broke so the free use of the St. Thomas campus church for student weddings was welcomed. Of course, we were only allowed to use the basement chapel. The person assigning use of the facility must have been a Tommie with a big class ring. In order to have a modicum of decor in enemy territory, I asked Fr. Don Talafous, then the college chaplain at St. John's, to perform the ceremony. Fr. Don stated that this was, as he saw it, a monumental occasion in ecumenical advancement.

Our marriage has been blessed, although the St. Thomas freebees from the State Fair usually end up in my bag. I tend to go to the Johnnie/Tommie game alone, so I can pace the sidelines, cheering on the Johnnies to beat those dreaded Tommies.

Dorms

Dorm life can make or break a person when college is the first great escape for a young adult. Dorms leave a lasting impression. At St. John's, the dorm most impressionable for freshmen was the 4th floor of Benet Hall. The building was built in the 1920s but it felt like it was out of the nineteenth century.

There were some 100 steps to climb up to get to the 4th floor. A service elevator was available, but it was not to be used except for moving in and out or for parents visiting.

Nobody ever found him or herself lost up on 4th Benet. The rooms were five plus feet wide, I could almost touch both walls at the same time. One window opposite a door with a transom, two metal clothes lockers, a bunk bed, two desks, two chairs and a sink. Plaster walls over clay tile blocks and a square linoleum tile floor on top of squeaking wood floor joists.

Benet Hall had the convenience of being connected to the refectory by an early version of a skyway, looking like something out of a medieval castle. Woe to the person who forgot a book and had gone all the way down, just to have to walk all the way back up and then all the way back down again. We were told it was an honor to be a resident on that floor, but no one took that seriously. It did build character, going up and down. You just did it, time and time again. You lost weight living with the original stair exercise program.

After my freshman year, I was ready for a ground level room and that was in St. Thomas Hall, the first floor. It was a standard, modern, two-person dorm room; closet, large window and boring. I have to admit, that year was non-descript for me. Now I had to wear a jacket in the winter to get food at the dining hall and students used the hallway as a passageway to get around campus in order to stay out of the weather. There was a lot of hall traffic and occasional thefts. There wasn't the same *esprit de corps* there, but then most residents were sophomores and had lost the adventure of being freshmen.

My third year it was back to Benet Hall, but this time in the basement with its huge, cavernous rooms for three students. The sheer size allowed for unique decor. There was space for a refrigerator, table, easy chair, sofa, barn wood walls, beds not bunked and all manner of precious college possessions. It was a very quiet existence. No one in their right mind would go down into the dungeon of basement Benet.

Senior year meant being on top of the feeding frenzy for picking dorm rooms. The only quality place left was Frank House. It was built around 1900 and it was laid out like a home. There was a yard and a screened gazebo with all the screens ripped out. The fire escape made for discreet exists and entries.

There was an odd collection of students living there. People who lived in Frank House did graduate, but I don't know how. The rooms were large, three students each and again, it allowed for creative embellishments. There was even parking in back. Now you no longer had to transverse the campus after parking to get to your dorm or race from the highway to get the last spot open in the close parking lots. Frank House was just far enough away to keep others out who did not need to be there.

Spring came way too soon that senior year. It was time to leave, ready or not. How soon you forget the sweltering hot fall days and the freezing winter nights. Wind and bugs generally let themselves in at their own convenience. Spring for seniors is the time to pack it up for good, sell the ancient refrigerator and load your possessions in the car for the last time. In those days, we came as freshman with a few bags of clothes and personal effects; and as seniors, we left with about the same amount. The simple life of the Benedictines grew on you. You just don't need so much stuff.

      My fifth-year senior fall semester was spent student teaching in St. Cloud, so I found a room to rent by the St. Cloud campus. I suspect most of my fellow residents didn't know I was a Johnnie. It was a rental house.   We cooked, ate and lived by ourselves. No more excitement at every entry into a room, no late night conversations. It was uninspiring.

Another Side of Gagliardi

I came to St. John's like many young men of that time, with a chip on my shoulder. Although I had a good upbringing, I rebelled from family life. In 1969, John was about the same age as many of the players' parents and many of us saw him as a surrogate father. He knew all of us by name, he knew about sports, he never told us to pick-up our rooms and he was always ready with a smile and a conversation.

John had an optimistic outlook on life. I remember once being in the old gymnasium with John and some other students, which was built in 1901 and had wooden ceiling trusses over the basketball court. John asked if we thought he could shoot a basketball up through the trusses from the sideline and have it come down into the basket. A view from the floor suggested that would be impossible. John, with a grin on his face, took the basketball and with a two handed set-shot, straight from the 1940's, stepped forward and shot the ball.

Through the trusses the shot went, somehow missing all the supports and braces and it fell cleanly, clanging off the basketball rim. We retrieved the ball and he shot it again. Swish, the shot went in. We were in total disbelief. We challenged him to do it again, but he respectfully declined, knowing not to press his luck. He showed us that the impossible is possible. He also demonstrated that the winters at St. John's are long and dreary, necessitating strange activities to pass the time.

One of John's greatest assets is his gift of gab. He could entertain anyone, anywhere, at anytime with conversation. It was illuminating to listen to him talk. The best part of two-a-day football practices were the nightly film sessions where he would put us in the aisles laughing. It was better than watching Johnny Carson on the Tonight Show. He is a great public speaker and he uses his skills well.

In the spring of my senior year, the Warner Palestra was just being completed. Of the many reasons for it to be built, one was to help integrate the Johnnies and Bennies by providing a more co-educational friendly facility. It seemed like heresy but the forward thinking monks knew that to compete for new students the old ways had to change.

The old Rat Hall gymnasium likely never saw a woman visitor within its bowels. The main floor was rough enough on women. If a Bennie walked too close to the stands during a basketball game, she would be passed up in a not too dignified fashion. That old building was scary. Every freshman athlete learned the shower two-step. When taking a shower, as soon as you felt the water pressure change, you quickly stepped out of the way or risked getting scalded. Many a visiting team had injury added to insult by getting a hot water burn in the shower.

As a freshman, it took me months to get the courage to explore the handball courts on the level below the locker rooms. It wasn't until my sophomore year that I found out there was a one-lane bowling alley down there, hand set your own pins. I never saw a girl in the weight room or handball courts in Rat Hall in all my time there.

So when I was with a group of Johnnies wandering the new Warner Palaestra athletic facility and came upon a number of Bennies by a water fountain, we were taken aback. What were women doing in the hallowed halls of a Johnnie sport's venue!

We wanted to talk to them but we were not able to summon the courage. This happened just outside John's office and he came out to see what the commotion was about. He was quick to pick-up on our embarrassment and inability to deal with the women. He suggested we just go up and start talking to them. He had no takers so he embarrassed us even more by walking up to the fountain, taking a drink and talking to the Bennies.

When he returned, he told the befuddled men a truism, "It doesn't matter what you say, just say something, like 'How's the water?' No one ever remembers what was said first anyway. Then the ice is broken and nature will take over." If it weren't for insights like that, many a Johnnie might never have found the nerve to get married.

Drink

St. John's, like all schools of higher education, has alcohol consumption in and around the campus. I came to St. John's quite immature. My drinking experiences hadn't even started until the summer after my senior year in high school. I could comprehend the concept of inebriation, but I had not yet attained it.

I was most amazed during those first weeks of school with the continuous posting of signs on campus advertising keggers. This did not seem to be the appropriate behavior for a Christian school to be condoning, especially when a majority of students were minors. Soon my notion of college drinking was drinking to get drunk. That view and the view of many freshmen conflicted with the local German tradition. To locals, beer was a drink to be consumed for pleasure, at meals and at most social occasions. The mere sight of beer should not entice drunkenness but refreshment and camaraderie.

At that first kegger, across the Lake Watab bridge, I paid my dollar, took a plastic cup and downed a few beers. All the while watching the proceedings, discreetly from a distance. It was debauchery as only freshmen can do it, inhibition spiraling into madhouse hooliganism.

There was an ongoing series of keggers that fall, including a pre-med party at the St. Anna Ballroom. By then, I had mastered the art of getting drunk at college. The cardinal rule was to make sure you know when the bus left and to make sure you got on it.

After the first month or so, the freshmen diverged in drinking disposition, some continued to seek out the party life and some, like myself, started to shy away. Getting sick and being hung over just wasn't worth the prior night's enjoyment. Besides, you must have appeared to others as obnoxious and as stupid as everyone else had appeared to you.

The next step in college drinking is the off campus bars. But for St. John's students, because the local taverns were four miles away in St. Joseph, many of us never got to that level. Again, the strong local German influence fashioned beer as a social drink. The town bars would have whole families in them, kids running around with parents drinking to socialize, but not drinking to get drunk.

In time everyone made his or her own decision, party on or slow down. With that dichotomy I fit in with the quiet weekend crowd; alone, sober and walking the campus at night searching out non-drinking activities. I wouldn't say that I was a party pooper, but my alcohol consumption was minimal in college after that freshman fall semester.

My last semester was spent student teaching in St. Cloud. I moved off campus so I would be close to the school I taught at. After the football season ended, I would still head out daily to campus to visit and get a free meal. As quiet as it might seem on St. John's campus, it was worse in St. Cloud if you didn't bar hop. One night I set out to see what it would be like to drink a lot of alcohol in a bar and get drunk. With my previous years of being a teetotaler, it didn't take much to get me inebriated.

At a bar in St. Joseph, I sat for the evening and drank until closing. With the "motel or hotel" proclamation, I got up to drive back to St. Cloud, about fifteen miles away. I knew I was drunk and I knew I shouldn't drive and I knew enough people in St. Joseph so that I could have stayed overnight there, but I decided to drive home anyway.

I sat in the car and figured out a game plan. I would just follow a large semi-truck because they drove straight through

St. Cloud at night, slow and steady. That way I wouldn't run any stoplights, I would stay centered on the road and everything would go fine. So off I went. It took a long time behind a slow truck. I was checking everything over and over: speed, ok; distance behind truck, ok; centered in lane, ok; no police around, ok.

      I pulled up behind my St. Cloud residence, put the car in park and congratulated myself on a job well done. I turned the key to off and pulled it out. I pushed in the head light switch to turn them off, but it didn't budge. I pushed hard a second and third time, but still I couldn't budge it. I slammed it and still it would not budge. Could the switch be broken? I looked up and saw that there wasn't any light reflecting off the house from my headlights. Then I realized with nauseous terror that I had never turned on the headlights. I had driven all the way home with the lights off. By staying close to the truck with its running lights, I had not realized that my lights were off.

      Since then I have never, ever driven a car after drinking even a couple of drinks. I have also come to believe that there is a God and that he does take care of idiots like me.

Road Trip

The Pine Curtain, that theoretical divide between St. John's and the rest of the world, loomed large if you did not have a car on campus. There were buses to get to St. Benedict's or St. Cloud and back, but most Johnnies who wanted to get somewhere and did not have a car had to hitchhike. Dating a student at the St. Cloud School of Nursing had me putting in a lot of cold, late nights hitchhiking. By far, the best college adventures were automobile trips driven from campus in a car that you controlled.

On my 21st birthday, I received a gift from my father, a "spare change" savings account he had kept over the years. By then, it was over $1,000 and that was more than enough for a used car (in 1972). The car I purchased was a 1965 Rambler sedan, red and white. I remembered wondering why the used car salesman kept saying that there was no warranty on the car until a month later when the reverse gear went out. A creative use for sawdust. For the next year and a half I drove it without having to backup. Only once did I have to get out and push. That car and my life were in the same mode, don't worry about where you have been, keep on going forward.

The first road trip was during summer two-a-days. After a Saturday's practice, we ate and headed down to the Minnesota State Fair. When we gassed up in St. Cloud, we received a promotional set of plastic mixing bowls, which become known as the "stone hats," for reasons I will not get into. The fair at night is grand. My roommate Steve and I managed to talk two high school girls into riding in the Tunnel of Love, hoping for a kiss, but we were shut down. How embarrassing.

Tom, my other roommate, got talked into a "strong man" test of strength contest where you use a mallet to hit a board that will ring a bell with a metal slide. The carnival barker thought he had roped in a sucker. He didn't realize how strong Tom was, how unrestrained Tom could get or that he was the one being set up. On his first swing Tom heaved a mighty stroke, but stopped the mallet inches from the board. He then looked around at the crowd and gave an impish laugh. The barker now knew he had lost control of his game. In rapid succession Tom rang the bell a number of times. He later told me the trick is not how strong you are but to use the correct technique.

As we headed back to St. John's we stopped at a donut shop that had an all glass window front, very 1970s. At the counter, visible from the outside, I ordered some donuts and when I went to pay for them I found my wallet empty. I looked up in disbelief and walked out. The boys outside were laughing so hard they were falling out of the car.

Another road trip was to LaCrosse, Wisconsin, for a football game. I rode the team bus down and friends drove my car. Once the game was over I waved byc-byc to the team bus with all the sad sacks on it heading back to St. John's. They were the players who couldn't finagle other transport back and therefore could not spend Saturday night in LaCrosse.

Oh yes, the drinking age in Wisconsin then was 18 versus Minnesota's 21 and there were multiple bars on every block. The wide-eyed boys from Minnesota like me, who were not yet 21, were quite taken with this college town. A raccoon that didn't quite make it across the road, but did manage to take out the fuel pump when I hit it, highlighted that trip.

When I injured by left knee and had a full-length cast on it, I would drive the car by putting my leg with the cast across the front seat and extend my right leg over the cast. I could use my right foot to work the brake, but keeping steady pressure on the accelerator was difficult. I took one of my crutches apart and jammed the lower part into the seat to press down the accelerator.

One evening during a snowstorm as I was coming down the north entry into St. John's I encountered snowdrifts across the road. I could not turn around since I did not have a reverse and I did not want to stop the car and get stuck so far out, so I gunned the engine and plowed through the snowdrifts. I got through quite a few, but eventually the car lost speed and got hung-up on top of a large drift. I was able to hobble the short distance back to my dorm without much difficulty.

After an hour of sleep I was awaken by campus security, they told me to move the car or have it towed by the county. I was able to convince him to give some dorm mates and myself a ride out to the car and we were able to get the car back.

Oh, the joys of a college road trip.

The Johnnie Football Adage

     The dominant rule for football practice in the early 1970s at St. John's was "Don't hit the ground." That is such a common sense idea that it defies me that other coaches never figured it out or when told about it, never realized the significance of it. If you don't hit the ground during practice you are much less likely to get hurt and, therefore, much more likely to be healthy on game day. Makes sense to me.

     At the college level and even in high school, players know how to hit and make contact. You don't need to teach brute force at those levels, you need to focus on skill and technique. Friends on other college teams told me that they looked forward to game day because it was easier on their bodies then practice. What is the value of beating up a player at practice to " toughen them up" for the game when they could end up getting hurt and not even play in the game. As the beer commercial says, "Brilliant! Brilliant!"

     There was a Johnnie quip about hitting the ground. We practiced with regular football pants back then and if someone had dirty knees, we would tell them they were being a good Catholic, praying to their patron saint, Saint Shit. One would work extra hard to not fall down so to avoid being confronted with that tribute.

     The first precept to the rule is, "Practice at half speed." It's easier to avoid hitting the ground when running at half speed but that does not mean there isn't hitting going on. One can still get in a good pop without going full speed. By avoiding the ground, a player becomes more skilled at their assignment, develops balance and breaks the habit of falling down to complete a play.

I am not saying that players didn't get hurt at St. John's practices, but it was rare. One such rare occurrence happened my junior year when St. John's had one of those teams that was well balanced and had potential to win it all. We were halfway through the season, playing masterfully and getting giddy because everything was falling in place for a run at a national championship. It was during a warm up lap when one of our star players decided to jump up on someone's shoulder, messing around. In doing so he dislocated his own shoulder. John was fit to be tied when that player ended up being out for the year.

Although we were good that year, Division III teams do not have much depth and the loss of a great player is tough to overcome. We never were quite the same after that. We still finished 8-1, but in those days if you didn't win them all and with authority, you didn't get invited to be one of the four teams in the national playoffs. John had us practicing for a week or so after the last game of the season hoping for the call that didn't come. We knew we had the capability to play with the best, but it was not to be that year.

On occasion during practice, someone would decide it was time to kick the intensity up a couple of notches. That would usually occur on the last practice before the first game of the season. One year an all-conference defensive tackle decided he wanted to get pumped up for the next day's game.

"I'm coming hard" he says to me and "boom", he blows right past me. He knew the unwritten rule of not going full speed, but he felt he wasn't ready for the game and he wanted to get some hard hits in.

"What the hell are you doing?" I asked him. Then he says it again, telling me I better get physical because he is coming in at full speed. The next play he knocks me on my backside, giving me his game face as I stood up.

I knew he wasn't going to stop so I had to get intense quickly. I switched to game mode, like Han Solo firing up the Millennium Falcon to make a quick escape. The hair on my back was standing up, I was take taking quick, deep breaths, stretching out the best I could while standing up and trying not to look too wacky to the other players. The next play was a wide sweep and I hit a defensive back, knocking him down. Now I get the dirty look of "are you crazy."

The next play is a pass, just what the doctor ordered for a physical hit. As we lined up we gave each other the cold stare. I was ready. With the snap of the ball I jumped back into position. He was use to me being docile so he was slack in using his hands to keep me from getting to his body. I fired out and caught him on his hip. As I drove into him he lost his footing and became airborne. When I had him behind the quarterback I let him fly through the air. The offensive lineman's vernacular to describe that type of block is to "send him out for a cheap cup of coffee."

The second offense team was in a semi-circle behind us, watching the play. John got out of the way but a number of other players didn't and they got knocked down in Keystone Cop fashion. John came up to me and said, "Take it easy Bill, it's just practice!"

As I walked back to the huddle all embarrassed the defensive tackle pats me on the back, laughs and says, "Now I'm ready for Saturday."

Living the Nightmare

Every college student has the nightmare, where they wake up in the middle of the night in a cold sweat, believing they have missed a final. I had the occasion of living that nightmare. And of course it all started with a woman.

I had been dating a coed when our relationship started to cool. We met as freshmen and we both had the same "small town kid lost in the big city" syndrome, which is really pathetic since St. Cloud and St. John's are far from being large metropolitan areas. We were attracted to each other for that very reason and we matured together over time. But as it happens we grew apart and I was the one who got dumped. I didn't see it coming and then it was over.

I hung on for a while but to no avail. With broken heart I started my junior spring semester in a depressed condition and by mid-term I found myself failing all my classes. Being a Natural Science major meant classes in zoology, genetics and organic chemistry. Not easy classes! But the hardest class I was taking was fourth semester calculus.

The previous fall I had been injured and spent three weeks out of class. I was then taking a third semester calculus class and I never caught up academically. The teacher took pity on me with a passing grade, but I was not prepared for the next level.

By spring mid-term I smartened up and realized what a fix I was in. I plotted a rigorous timetable to catch up on what I had missed and at the same time try to stay up with the current class work. I had to learn that which I had not yet learned while trying to learn that which was now being taught, which was based on prior teaching.

About a day after midterms were posted, I received a visit from Gagliardi. He wanted to know what in the world was happening and why I was taking such a heavy class load. I assured him I would work it out but I suspected he started penciling in a new name on his line-up card. I became a bookworm and spent hours outlining and studying. Each day I put in a solid six plus hours of homework, studying late in the evenings and on weekends. But then without a girlfriend, it was much easier to find the time.

As I started to catch up it became evident I could not properly prepare all four classes, one was going to have to be ignored or all the classes would suffer. As I sat in the calculus class not understanding what was going on, it became apparent that this was the class that would be sacrificed.

I skipped some calculus classes but I would show up enough to let the teacher know I was still in the class. I hoped that somehow I could pull it out. I also was too proud and too dumb to drop the class. By the time spring finals came around, I had turned the corner and was doing well in all the other classes. But calculus had passed from my mind. Of course doing well is relative, to work up a failing grade at mid-term to just finish with a "C" takes an "A" or "B" in the second half.

I was very pleased with my accomplishments. I had outlined a large tome for each class and I knew all the material well. As each final's schedule was posted in class I wrote it down and took the finals. They all went well.

Then it happened, I had the nightmare. On my last night on campus I jumped up in a cold sweat from the bed and ran to my desk to check the school bulletin for the complete schedule of all class finals. Since I had not gone to the calculus class for a while, I had not written down the date of the final. The school bulletin listed the calculus final test day for my section as having already passed. My plan had been to take the final and hope for the best, but now even that was not possible.

The aftermath of the "missed final nightmare" is that after a while you're not really sure you really did forget to take the test, that maybe you just dreamed you forgot to take the test and that you actually did take the test. When the final grades were mailed out, the "F" as my calculus grade made it quite obvious that I had indeed missed that final.

I was still able to keep my grades up above the athletic suspension level even with the one failing grade. That next fall when I showed up for football, I still had a starting position. John greeted me back with a big grin.

Missed Dreams

      The desire to excel in sports is the driving force for most athletes. As one improves his or her level of play, skills develop and aspirations for more success increase. The goal is to play better at the next level. For college players that means playing professional. Not that all players have that as their objective, but it is in the back of their minds somewhere.

      The thought of playing professional football was not one I entertained when I first went to St. John's. There was a small but steady stream of professional scouts that would stop in for a visit with John. They had the boonies scouting circuit, hitting St. John's on their way to or back from the Dakotas, Montana and northern Minnesota.

      My only attribute was speed, I was fleet of foot. When the scouts would be timing the prospects in the forty-yard dash, John would call me over and tell the scout "This kid is real fast." I usually didn't disappoint but with my lack of bulk I was just a curiosity. Over the years the scouts would ask to see that fast kid again, hopping I had bulked up. I hadn't, but I stayed fast.

      By my last year at St. John's, the scout's interests in me had finally turned my head. I was about to graduate and I had the looming decision of getting a teaching job and settling down in some small town or playing for a professional team, make a lot of money and travel all over the country. Not much of a choice!

Money in those days was relative, neither a teacher nor a professional player made much. A professional player then would make maybe three times that of a teacher, not an inordinate amount. In today's world one would be foolish not to try to play professional if given the chance. It's too lucrative a salary to pass up, 10 to 20 times that of a teacher.

I received a letter in mid November 1973 from the Dallas Cowboys asking me to fill in a questionnaire about where I would be and how to contact me in the next few months. I was exhausted from student teaching, playing football, not winning and going though a very cold and snowy winter. I stated in the return portion that I didn't know where I would be in the next few months, but wherever I was, it would be warm. Not a smart thing to do.

I ended up in Arizona, living off a fellow Johnnie, working out with renewed vigor. Sunshine and warm weather in January to someone just out of snow country is the ticket to restored vitality. The draft came and went and I was flabbergasted that I was not picked. With dejected ego I started on a long hitchhiking trip through the west, going to California, Canada and eventually arriving at St. John's in the late spring of 1974.

By then, I was in very poor shape. I had not been eating well nor working out. I visited with John and the first thing he said was, "What in the world did you tell the Dallas Cowboys? They were going to draft you!" The consequences of my flippant attitude were now painfully evident.

But then a little luck came into play. The National Football League in the spring of 1974 had a players' strike looming and there was renewed interest in Division III players to help fill team rosters.

Within a day or so I got a call from the Dallas Cowboys. I apologized for my prior communication, blaming it on winter brain freeze. They seemed to understand and then offered to fly me down to Dallas to sign a contract. Almost immediately I received a second call from the Green Bay Packers, they also wanted me to sign a contract. I stated I had already verbally agreed to sign with Dallas, but then they offered a signing bonus of $500. My Scottish blood must have kicked in, for although that was not a lot of money even then, it was a whole lot more then I had in my pocket.

I was in a quandary so I went to John. He advised that with the Cowboys, who were the top team in the NFL at that time, one would have a tough time getting on the team. Whereas the Packers, who were sliding from their prior dominance, one would have a better chance of making the team. With that advice I took the money and started working out full time. After a few months I was at the top of my game. I was in the best shape of my life, gained 25 pounds and I had an airplane ticket to Green Bay in hand.

I went to the local high school to have one more workout before flying out to Green Bay's football camp the next day. I was reluctantly talked into a pick-up basketball game so I figured I would just run wind sprints up and down the court and pretend to be playing. On one sprint down the court the ball passed over my head, I instinctively jumped to grab it, landed awkwardly and felt my knee snap.

Funny things happen in life and just that fast, dreams are gone. The doctor thought it would heal but it didn't and an operation would not help. With much disappointment, I got on with life and by fall I was teaching high school science in a small town.

But I got the money. It was the easiest thing I have ever done to make money. Just sign a piece of paper and get paid to do that, which I would have gladly paid someone else for. To have the chance to play professional football.

Benedictine Bad Boys

Although this piece is written with humor, I must first state that all deviant sexual behavior is reprehensible. I offer this chapter as a view of how I saw it when I was growing up. God be with all victims.

As with most children in the 1950s and 1960s I knew nothing about deviant sexual behavior. I barely knew what sex was. Calling someone who was different than me "Queer!" "Homo!" or "Faggot!" was just a way to express an insult. I had no idea what it meant. That was during a time when one didn't expect to encounter changes from normal behavior and when variations did occur you looked the other way.

In Catholic grade school I never quite knew what to make of nuns; male, female, or something in-between. In seventh grade I worked sweeping out the schoolrooms after school. It was then that I learned after cleaning the nuns' bathroom that they were indeed women. Nuns, however domineering, never were a physical threat except for the occasional ruler whack across the knuckles.

Around eighth grade on a hot summer's night while roaming my hometown's streets I happened upon a discussion between some friends about odd goings on at the past summer's scout camping trip. One of the boys told the story about how he was offered the honor of sleeping in the tent of the scout leader. During the night he felt a hand reaching over him going towards his privates. He cupped his hands over such and turned away.

The more reaching there was the harder he hung on and twisted away. Eventually the reaching stopped, but he didn't sleep that night.

Suddenly the fellow talking was slapped up side the head by another boy. "Why didn't you tell me that before I spent the night in the tent with the leader! I had to do the same thing!" They had a laugh about it and slugged each other in feint anger. Then simultaneously and in serious tone, they talked about the one boy who spent the balance of the camping trip in the leader's tent and how he and the leader had recently moved away.

That conversation likened to silly pranks played out by boys. It must have been, however, a devastating encounter for that other boy who likely has suffered the rest of his life.

In Catholic high school, I learned about religious brothers, who were not to be messed with. They were younger than the nuns and were not afraid to slam you into a locker for most any reason. Unlike parish priests who were all older and generally dying off, the brothers seemed to be carrying heavy loads and were edgy all the time. That played out when they left the religious life in great numbers in later years. By the end of high school I had a healthy respect for the religious. Avoid confronting them at all costs.

At St. John's there were priests, brothers, and monks, yet it was different then before. They were a functioning community in their own private world. You entered their domain and you felt their command. It quickly became known that there were some men of the cloth that you needed to watch out for, whom supposedly would use their power for their own ends. There were rumors about particular religious persons and that was sufficient for me to steer clear. It was sad, but a healthy dose of pessimism served me well. In an awkward situation when I didn't feel comfortable, I would just get up and walk out of the room.

Thirty years later, when the sexual abuse scandal broke at St. John's, the rumored names appeared in print. The hearsay was true.

Those things were not talked about in polite society back then. Not that people didn't think it couldn't exist, but credence would not be given to it, so people likely would not have acted even if someone did come forward. A person of the cloth then was above reproach and some used that to their advantage.

Today society has evolved to a point where nothing is sacred and that is for the better. If there had been less fear and embarrassment back then, people would have spoken up and stopped the initial assaults before it had an opportunity to continue. The pain today is great because the abuse was allowed to fester and grow. If only the perpetrators had been stopped in their tracks back then like more are today, so much suffering would have been avoided.

Injuries

If there had been an award for being injured I would have been an All-American. I never completed a full season, either someone else got injured and that gave me a chance to play or I got injured and that gave another a chance to play. Some injuries just happen, but for me, they were from mental mistakes made while playing. Being human means making mistakes and I had my fair share of miscues that resulted in injuries.

One year St. John's was playing the reigning conference champion late in the season and both teams were looking forward to being the conference champion. A lot was riding on the game and it was homecoming for us on a bitterly cold day. On the last play of the first half as I was running down field to throw a block I made a mistake. I could not quite reach my assignment so instead of pulling up I threw a cross-body block. John doesn't teach cross-body blocking and he later let me know that explicitly. As I was flying through the air my intended target saw me coming and lowered his helmet into the side of my chest. I heard a crack when we made contact.

When playing in freezing weather the cold numbs pain. You don't want to warm up because then the pain will come. I played the third quarter, but late in the fourth quarter I took myself out. I could hear sloshing in my chest. I didn't think much about it after the game when getting ready to go to the homecoming dance. As I met my date and gave her a hug a terrific pain shot through my chest. Then a miraculous and most non-masculine thing happened. I looked her in the eyes and said, "I've got to go to the hospital!"

I passed out in a friend's car before we ever got to the hospital and I awoke in a wheel chair in the middle of a vomiting session. It took me a long time to recover from a punctured lung.

The next year at about mid season, we were playing St. Thomas at our homecoming and we were holding onto a narrow lead late in the fourth quarter. That is when you need to play smart, concentrate and do not think about the upcoming homecoming dance. Just finish the game. On a pass play as I dropped back to block the defensive lineman stunted in. I was not focused and I had not positioned myself properly. I pivoted on my outside leg to block him down the line of scrimmage instead of blocking him to the outside.

With that poor pass blocking technique and with minimal if any contact, my knee ripped out. Down I went like a pile of bricks, my knee was a blob of jelly. With a knee operation and 20 pounds of plaster, I ended up spending the next six weeks on crutches and then months in the training room.

After two season-ending injuries I was told by one of my roommate that if I got hurt the next year and didn't finish the season, John would have to shoot me like an old horse to put me out of my misery.

That final season I was living off campus, student teaching seven hours a day plus playing football; my life was very hectic. We were in a losing effort when a two-guard pulling play was called. Now I am sure it was called to the right, but the other guard was sure it was called to the left. As I pulled out I saw his helmet heading for my head so I stood up quickly. Whack, his helmet went into my shoulder. The pain was immediate and I ended up with a partially separated shoulder. I sat out the next game but remembering the words of my roommate, I played the last two games with a donut pad on my shoulder. I was minimally effective which matched how the team played. We lost those games, but at least John didn't have to put me out of my misery.

To this day when we meet I mention to that fellow player that he went the wrong way. But then I give him the benefit of the doubt since he was an All-American.

Sex and the Lonesome Johnnie

    I grew up a normal male teenager. I thought about sex at least once a minute, probably the national norm. I wasn't a choirboy but I did get through those years without too much trouble. There are a number of embarrassing moments which are best left quiet, else I lock myself in a closet and never come out.

    The philosophy I developed for myself for dealing with the opposite gender was that of respect. Respect for the woman and respect for myself. In the nomenclature of baseball I knew my way around the bases, but I never got to home plate until after I graduated from St. John's. I could put on the charm, yet when the woman made it known that things had gone as far as she wanted, I stopped. Respecting the other person gives a proper outlook on personal relationships. Like the John Wayne retort of, "I treat others fairly and I expect to be treated the same." That was my rule.

    Respecting yourself is important. You respect yourself by not putting yourself in a situation that could potentially harm you. A few years out of college, I was on a date when things heated up. I asked the woman if she wanted to have sex and she said yes. Then I blurted out, "I don't think so!" The reality was that I did not know her well and I was not in a position to accept any remote consequence of pregnancy and its responsibility. We never went out again. She must have thought I was one strange person. It was respect for myself that kept me out of a potentially bad situation, even if the flesh was more than willing.

There is a small man-made lake in St. Cloud called Lake George that had a lighted fountain in the center, a superb place to go parking on a date. One spring when my parents were visiting and taking my date and I out to dinner, I pointed out the lake as we drove by.

"I bet that's a good place to watch submarine races," my mother said off-handedly. I had no idea what she was talking about. My date was beet red and elbowing me to be quiet as I persisted with asking how submarines would even fit much less race in such a small body of water. Luckily my mother was smart enough to know when her son is clueless and when best to drop the conversation before it gets even more embarrassing. Later that night after my parents had left, I was informed by my date about submarine races—another way to say necking.

Thanksgiving one year, while my roommates and I were packing up to leave on our separate ways for the long weekend, there was a knock at the door of our room. A beautiful Bennie that I did not know was standing there asking if I wanted to go home with her for the long weekend. Things like that just don't happen to me. I could barely mumble that my bag was already packed as I followed her out to her car in total bewilderment.

I was apprehensive about going to a woman's home for an overnight, but her parents were very open-minded and this activity seemed perfectly normal to them. We had dinner and conversation and when it was time to go to bed I was put in the basement guestroom. I got ready for bed and turned on the television. After a while the Bennie walks into the room in her pajamas, closes the door and sits on the bed next to me.

I was flabbergasted; I did not know what to do. I decided virtue was the best course of action so I didn't start any patty cakes. We talked until it got late and then I told her I was going to bed. She got up and as she walked out the door she looked back at me with a dumbfounded look.

When I was back at school I related the story and was promptly made the fool. I was laughed at for missing an opportunity for a wild weekend tryst.

That next fall I asked her out for a date to see what it was that I might have missed. We ended up at Lake George and as things were progressing she put her hand on my hand that was perched on her body, looked straight into my lustful eyes with her sparkling ones and said, "I found Jesus."

Well that can kill the mood real quick. Since I had started out with bad intentions I thought it best to suffer the consequences quietly. I congratulated her and we spent the rest of the evening discussing religion. Not the most memorable date.

Zen and the Art of Blocking

The key to being a good offensive lineman is to know you have the best job on the team even though everyone else thinks you have the worst. A defensive lineman can be a hero if he makes only one big play in a game, but an offensive lineman is the goat if he makes just one bad play in a game. As with life, your attitude makes all the difference in how you perform. By believing you have the best position on the team and that you wouldn't want any other, you play your best.

One basic tenet in football is that there are two types of players, the hitters and the hittees. Being afraid of hitting and allowing your opponent to get their whacks in on you makes for a long and painful practice or game. I was a hittee when I was a freshman on the St. John's scrub (practice) squad, letting the starting defensive unit get their hits on me.

It's not that you need to hit someone as hard as you can; you just need to make the first contact to be the hitter. That way you control the play and it also hurts a whole lot less. In the first game I played in, a chiseled, Atlas-type defensive player with fifty pounds over me was continuously pile-driving me into the ground, play after play. The next year I got my shoulder pad on him before he could grab me and I drove him all over the field.

The key to blocking from a three-point stance is to be balanced on your feet so that you can go in any direction. The hand on the ground is for appearance only. In high school I would put my weight forward and drive dirt into my finger joints. They would get infected and I would look like a Neanderthal. If you are going to be able to go in any direction without giving the defensive player a tell, every stance has to look the same. One has to work at that, getting into the same stance position to pull right, pull left, drive ahead and pass block. Practice, practice, practice the same look.

Another basic rule of blocking is that "the low man wins." Being a tall player I was generally picked to do the "low-man wins" demonstration on the first day of practice. My opponent would be the shortest player on the team. Gagliardi would gather everyone in a large circle and have me stand straight up with the other player in a proper blocking position. On "go" I would be pushed back in quick order. When it was my turn to block John would get a big laugh out of the crowd with me lined up in the proper position and the other player about to get hammered. Then John would stop the demonstration and tell everyone to go back to the drill. He would tell me that he didn't want to hurt anybody, but just once I wanted to get in my block!

I took John's advice to heart. I had such poor upper body strength that I could not stand up and do battle with a defensive lineman. My power was quickness, staying low and never leaving my feet. I tried hard to not look like a walrus during mating season when blocking.

The proper driving block is as simple as putting your shoulder pad on the hip of your opponent. Like the sweet spot on a golf club, if you hit it just right, the result is amazing. The trick to making proper contact is quickness and the trick to quickness is being relaxed. Do not tense up in anticipation of impact. You must explode like a sprinter, relaxing opposite muscle groups and drive through the opponent.

Pass blocking is more like boxing. Don't let the defensive person get his hands on you. As he reaches out deflect his hands. Pop him in the chest with your shoulder pads, back off and do it again. Always keep your opponent to the outside. John had a great shtick for players that would stay in one spot and pass block by standing up and trying to push their opponent backwards. He called it the "Jane Mansfield block." It was quite humorous to see him demonstrate it, hands clasped on his chest, elbows sticking straight out as he walked about mimicking a buxom beauty.

Be that what it may, I admit I did like the Jane Mansfield block for down-field blocking assignments. When I tried to block a defensive halfback in the open field I generally got more dirt than opponent. The Jane Mansfield block worked well to corral in the opponent and then run over them.

By making blocking, a mundane activity, into a highly skilled art form, you learn to conquer that and any other task in life, however dreary.

Good Deeds

Even at a Catholic school, finding Christians can be a challenge. St. John's was no different. The students were into their own world and charity to others was not always forthcoming. "Why get involved" is deeply ingrained in most college students. I would quickly walk past the tables with papers on them that were set up around campus. They usually wanted some type of volunteer action or commitment. Not making eye contact worked for me.

One day in the refectory, a fellow Johnnie pointed out a remarkably good looking woman behind a table and he mentioned that she was a schoolmate of ours from grade school, a few years younger than us. The little whelp that was loud and obnoxious then had become all grown up with piercing eyes and remarkable beauty.

I walked up and introduced myself and before I knew it I was signed up to be a Big Brother. Will I ever learn! My little brother and I did the usual Harlem Globetrotters thing with the organization and then we started to hang out together. I never considered myself very interesting and I suspect he didn't either. We never really talked much. I ended up being transportation for his various errands.

I took him out bowling one Saturday and when we got to the lobby he stopped to watch a foosball game. At that time foosball games were all the rage. They are quarter-sucking machines in lobbies that have two pairs of participants playing against each other. You twisted handles with pegs on them that looked like soccer players over a table trying to score a goal with a small hard ball.

I asked if he would like to play and he said sure so I put a quarter on the table and we waited our turn. Now this kid was maybe twelve and he came from a broken home so I assumed he didn't know how to play foosball. It was more of an adult game and where would he get the money and opportunity to play?

Within a few minutes, it was obvious that he was far my superior at playing the game. I had started in back to control the game; however, we quickly switched positions so he could run the attack. I eventually lifted up my men to just get out of his way.

You know a good foosball player by the sound the ball makes when hitting the back of the goal on a kill shot. If it rattles around you're a wimp, if it makes a sharp thud—you got game. He wiped out all of the competition until some seasoned college players beat us. Being a good foosball player is like being a good pool player, it's a sign of a miss-spent youth.

On another visit, I took him and one of his friends out to ride a mini-motor bike in some open fields. I sat in the car for an hour or so until they came back. I noticed they had a small sack with them when they returned that I had not noticed when they left. I didn't think much about it until the next day when I read in the newspaper about some home break-ins in the area where we had been. I never brought up the topic with him but it was obvious that this kid was much more worldly than I.

We kept seeing each other over the school year. In the spring I started getting calls from his mother about her ex-husband who was harassing her. She wanted me to come over and beat him up. I don't think so. It was then that I called the "old classmate" and we decided it would be best for me to stop seeing the kid.

I may not have been an effective big brother but I tried.

Winning in Perspective

    I was unaware of the winning tradition at St. John's when I first went there. For me, St. John's was just a place to go to keep playing sports after high school. Division III college athletics is that level where many good high school athletes can go to keep playing and to stay involved in competition. Division I college athletics is that level where only the best of the best are able to compete. Sport is a business at that level and there is the real possibility of eventually playing as a professional. My knowledge of college sports, while in high school, was minimal. I had no idea that one of the great small college winning traditions existed at St. John's.

    By the time two-a-day practices were over my freshman year, I knew where I was. It was discovered by watching old game films and listening to John's stories, not by some proclamation. Then you knew you were in a place where winners come from. At St. John's you quickly ascend to that ideal of expecting to be a winner.

    The strength of St. John's program isn't the number of games won, the win-loss record is just the end result. It's the understanding that having a winner's attitude is what makes for winning. Some teams win games but they never have a winner's attitude. You may not win every game, but you can have a winner's attitude in every game and that's the true goal. A winning attitude is what you should take away when you are done with athletics. Having a large tally of victories becomes shallow the moment you leave the college campus.

I have to admit that some of us looked forward to the possibility of playing professionally. It was a pipe dream as I look back at it. Division III has no scholarships so the players play for the fun of sport. It's athletics for now not for the future. The attention of scouts was an honor, but they are only looking for that rare prospect under the radar of all the other nationally known players. If your head got too swollen from the attention, your fellow teammates were more than willing to kick you back to reality.

In Division III competitive athletics is over with graduation. You finish out your career as a collegian. When you leave campus you leave the playing field. You may have stayed in shape and active past college, but that is just the natural progression of what you are, an athlete.

I admit I didn't understand the wining attitude philosophy as soon as I should have. As a young parent I initially was the obnoxious father in the stands at my children's youth sporting events. I eventually realized the gift I had received and then I taught a winning attitude when my time came to coach my children's teams.

What I had learned at St. John's I found well written in a letter from Theodore Roosevelt to his son in 1903.

> I am delighted to have you play football. I believe in rough, manly sports. But I do not believe in them if they degenerate into the sole end of any one's existence. I don't want you to sacrifice standing well in your studies to any over-athleticism; and I need not tell you that character counts for a great deal more than either intellect or body in winning success in life. Athletic proficiency is a mighty good servant, and like so many other good servants, a mighty bad master... A man must develop his physical prowess up to a certain point; but after he has reached that point there are other things that count more... [D]on't ever get into the frame of mind which regards these things as constituting the

end to which all your energies must be devoted, or even the major portion of your energies.

(Courtesy Theodore Roosevelt, edited by Joseph Bucklin Bishop, *Theodore Roosevelt's Letters to His Children* p. 63-65 New York: Charles Scribner's Sons, 1919).

That is a good summary of how athletics should be positioned in one's life and a good description of what Division III athletics is all about.

To Reno in a Torino

Some people have a fancy for adventure and I am one of them. I love to take off for far away places on short notice. I am not reckless, my rules are to be in control of my situation, make quality decisions, don't take chances if they appear to be less than sound and be wary of the easy way. That being said being 6'5" and 225 pounds was my best asset. But even that was not taken for granted.

In the 1970s, the generally later Easter Break made trips from northern colleges were rejuvenating because winter was almost over at the start and when you returned spring had sprung. Today with Winter Breaks generally in mid winter you return to winter. Winters at St. John's can be best depicted by a Gagliardi witticism, "The weather is clear and still," meaning snow is clear up to your butt and still coming down.

One Easter Break I planned to take a trip out west. It was to be with a fellow Johnnie and a friend from high school but at the last minute the Johnnie backed out. Another Johnnie learned of the predicament and asked if he could go instead. There needed to be three bodies to rotate driving shifts in order to drive straight through so he was in.

We started off from St. Paul in a 1970 Ford Torino with a 302 engine and a four gear standard shift on the floor. Not five minutes out the Johnnie asked what the third pedal on the floor was for. The high school friend and I looked at each other and groaned. Was it going to be that for the next four thousand miles and ten days, only two of us would be driving? On the Johnnie's first turn at driving I sat next to him and worked the stick, gas and clutch while he steered. He was a quick study and soon he was driving on his own.

Now the Johnnie must have made some sort of blood pact with his parents that he would not partake in the usual vices associated with a road trip. He did not go drinking or carousing, however, he did watch us with his eyes wide open, a sort of "country boy meets the seedy side of life" scenario. My high school friend and I were not social deviants, but the Johnnie did have a number of chuckles at our misadventures.

Our target was Reno, actually Lake Tahoe, where a cousin of mine was working, to see the bright city lights. But once we were there, it was clear there were no bright lights in Lake Tahoe so we pressed on to San Francisco. We would drive to a motel, have the Johnnie who was the smallest hide in the back seat, pay for a two-person room and then cut cards to see who got to sleep on the floor.

San Francisco is audacious even for the adventurous. My high school friend and I decided we wanted to see naked women dancing, but the Johnnie would have none of that. He stayed in a sleazy cafe on the waterfront while we looked for a bar with naked woman. It wasn't a long search, just next door. We walked in and sat down.

Now I was expecting to see something out of a Playboy magazine, a male college student's most fanciful fantasy: women all over, generously proportioned, vivacious, titillating on the stage and naked. The place stunk of stale beer and you could barely see through the choking cigarette smoke. There was a petite, naked woman on the stage dancing to taped psychedelic music. The woman was so skinny that it was hard to tell if she was in fact a female. Her expression was that of an addict nervously killing time in anticipation of her next fix. The place was pathetic.

The waitress came over and put down four draft beers on the table and said, "That will be five dollars." Now in the early 1970s a draft beer in the Midwest would run 50 cents and at happy hour down to a nickel in some places. I said we only wanted one each but was informed it was a two-drink minimum.

Our naiveté was thoroughly obvious. I gave her a five-dollar bill and she quickly said "Each." The high school friend handed over a second five-dollar bill.

"Each beer!" she said, getting more frustrated. We looked at each other in disbelief, this foray into the immoral side was getting quite expensive. We made a quick glance to the door but there were two large bouncers standing there. Not going to try to bolt. We paid up and returned our attention to the dancer.

After a while it became obvious that she was all the entertainment there was going to be, no other voluptuous beauties were standing at the stage entrance waiting to come out and entertain. The music and dancing never varied, it became quite boring and not a bit sexually exciting, yet the people in there appeared to be enjoying it. We eventually realized that our situation was hopeless so we cut our losses and left.

Back at the cafe we found the Johnnie very distraught. It seemed a couple of sailors had tried to pick him up and he had put a death grip on the table so they could not get him out. He was ready to die at that booth before leaving with them. We related our misadventure and we all had a good laugh.

After a few days of driving some 1,800 miles straight through, we were back at school enjoying the spring air and looking for new adventures.

A Lesson from Sports

Sport is a great teacher of life lessons. Regardless of the nature of the athletic endeavor, one learns important perspectives of life from competition that carries over for the rest of life. Sport is not just the thrill of victory and the agony of defeat; it is setting goals, working hard and accepting outcomes. Being a winner is not about going undefeated. Being a winner is about never giving up.

When I was at college, Gagliardi was St. John's football, literally. He ran and did everything that dealt with football. There was one assistant, Terry Haws, who in his own right was a top caliber coach. But Terry kept a low profile. His contribution was generally limited to saying, "That's right, John." He was there to enjoy the ride, to be part of the unique system at St. John's.

In my view everyone got a chance at St. John's. It may have been by waiting your turn through the years, by being called into a game out of the blue or by just a serendipitous opportunity in practice to show your skill. Chances occurred but they weren't overt. John had an eye for talent even if you didn't know you had it.

Football is a sport that operates within a pecking order. Lots of bodies on the sidelines but only eleven on the field at a time, you have to be patient and wait it out. Sometimes you wait and wait and never get the call. As freshmen it is rare to play. As sophomores only the best get to play but opportunities start occurring as the season wears on. If you are not playing by the end of your junior year it can be tough to move up as a senior. During my sophomore year, my opportunity happened at practice when a starting lineman got hurt and I was abruptly standing with the first team running plays.

I was in big trouble. I hadn't memorized the playbook as well as I should have. I had been too comfortable going through the second team motions, waiting for my turn next year. It became obvious to John that I was not prepared. He tested our preparedness by having us stand at our position as he called out plays in a rapid succession. Everyone had to point out and call out their blocking assignment and I didn't know mine. I looked the fool, tears welled in my eyes. The other linemen tried to cover for me, but I got pulled out and others were put in. As it turned out, no one was prepared to earn that position on that day.

I was humiliated and I could have assumed defeat at that point. I returned to my dorm room and studied the playbook late into the night. I was prepared the next day. Nevertheless, would I get another opportunity? John was trying different people and no one was up to it. Finally, with desperation in his voice, he asked if I was ready to play the position. I would be the fool once, but not twice. I was ready and I secured that starting job.

It didn't always happen that way. One player on the team was a quarterback with a cannon for an arm, who became a good friend over the years. He had been a hero in high school, once throwing two touchdowns passes late in a homecoming game to win it. His one weakness was speed, he had none. He worked harder than anyone did, but he never did get the call. Many of us had talked to John about giving him a chance. It just wasn't in the cards.

Every year he came to camp well prepared. By his senior year he had assumed the role of running the opponent's defense for the offense to go against, making use of his considerable football knowledge. Then at one practice John suddenly found himself without any quarterbacks. They were either hurt or sick. As John called out his name the seniors realized that he was finally getting an opportunity, even though it wasn't likely he would earn the job. In serious overtones and with a death grip on their jerseys, the seniors grabbed and advised the underclassmen that if they dropped any passes thrown to them, to keep running because we would be coming after them.

The running plays went well but on the first pass he threw a duck. The more he passed the more it was apparent that he had not spent those long mundane hours throwing during the summer, preparing for the season. The next day the regular quarterbacks were back and the opportunity was gone. Certainly there was no way he would have broken into the starting lineup based on one day's showing, but if he had sparkled, it would have made John reconsider whether or not he had made the right decision years earlier.

The lesson was learned; be prepared, work hard and don't give up. Whether you ever get the opportunity to play or not isn't the point, being prepared is. That's for the rest of your life. My friend and I have learned that lesson and it serves us well to this day.

Be Here Now

The greatest life lesson I learned at St. John's I learned before I knew how to describe it. It was the summer of my senior year at St. John's when I lived in Squaw Valley, California, where I read a book on Timothy Leary that gave me the defining expression, "Be Here Now."

As all college students have experienced there is a great loneliness and silence that becomes one while you are away from home. At St. John's there was the potential in the 1960s and 1970s that it could be with you for four years, since there wasn't ever-present entertainment to depend on. At that time St. John's offered minimal campus recreation, an occasional kegger, Friday movies and infrequent dances. The loneliness could not be masked. A number of Johnnies quickly became suitcase weekenders, hitting the road by 3:00 P.M. on Friday and not returning until 7:00 P.M. on Sunday.

As a freshman I initially equated St. John's quiet and solitude as boredom. Being from a suburb of the Twin Cities I was used to being entertained and I now had to learn how to entertain myself. In time, the quiet and solitude of St. John's became a very good friend.

A majority of students stayed the weekends on campus and battled the perceived boredom. It was tough at first, walking from one side of campus to the other and back again. Exploring all the paths on campus and in the woods and inevitably ending up at Mary Hall Commons student union a couple of times a night to watch foosball or a pool game or see who was there. The quiet could be deafening, it could bring tears to your eyes. The monotony could be never ending; you always wanted to be somewhere else and you found yourself just killing time until anything new would come to pass, which rarely did. The more you fought it the worse it got. I was in a freshman funk.

It was at the start of my sophomore year when I was enlightened. I was again dreading the upcoming year, trying to figure how I was going to get through the semester as fast as possible. I was not content with the present. I just tolerated it. Then it came to me as I was staring out of my dorm window on a bight fall day. Enjoy, because it's great to just *be*. This is the greatest time of my life because I am *here*. Don't sulk and long for things to get better; delight in the situation you find yourself in *now*.

From that point on, I looked forward to every minute of my time at St. John's with gusto. Time passed quickly because it was satisfying. I was no longer jealous of the suitcase weekenders, they were the ones who were missing out. The next three years went by quickly. There was much to do and I set out to do all that I could. The greatest gift from St. John's for many students is to have received this enlightenment.

My roommate Tom asked if I wanted to go with him to pick up a returning priest at the airport in Minneapolis, a five-hour round trip at 5:00 p.m. on a Sunday night in mid-winter. Another student who had volunteered decided he did not want to waste his time and talked my roommate into doing the task. I told him that he was duped, but he responded that actually the other fellow was duped because the other fellow would miss out on being with him while he was carrying out the task. With such logic, I could not argue so I agreed to go along.

It was a long and rewarding evening. The priest was an ancient language scholar and as unexciting as that may sound, the conversation that night never slowed down. In addition, he gave both of us a copy of a book that he had just translated from a Greek mythology tale. I didn't want the night to end.

That is a classic example of "Be Here Now." Mr. Leary was into drugs and had other ideas that I did not find particularly noteworthy, but that ideal for inner peace was exactly right. To have contentment with yourself, you have to accept the moment, no matter the circumstances. Times will get better and times will get worse so be happy with your current situation and you will master your environment.

That's not saying everything is always grand, that's not realistic, but it made the quiet times at St. John's much more pleasant and relaxing. I no longer fretted about the lack of activity or worried about how the future would be better. The present was good enough, whatever it was.

More Than a Game

When I came to St. John's in 1969, John Gagliardi had already made a name for himself in college football. Although he would take St. John's to unparalleled heights in football during the following years, when I first showed up, he had already accomplished more then most coaches ever will.

The goal then, as I suspect it is now, is to win every game. One loss puts a damper on the season. In my day the national championship was a four team playoff. You not only had to be undefeated, you had to be dominant. Some accused John of beating up on opponents, he didn't. He was trying to gain recognition for his teams, not running up the score. When his teams were playing great football the points just kept coming.

John claimed that the greatest team he had up to that time was the 1962 squad: "Undefeated. Untied. Uninvited." The 1963 and 1965 teams were also undefeated but they won national championships. The seasons after those distinguished years were somewhat less then stellar and John noted that although the teams had developed character, they needed to spend more time on developing winning ways. He has had both the character and the winning ways going strong ever since.

A great mind is always looking for a new way to accomplish usual tasks. John's gift to football was simplifying the basics. To emphasize an idea he would make up a taut phrase to help focus on the point.

"Apply the pad." That was a phrase for blocking. It didn't matter about all the techniques, huffing, yelling and pumping your feet; just get the shoulder pad on the opponent and push him out of the way.

"Minor detail." Everything was a minor detail when compared to the ultimate goal of winning the game. Determining who goes on which bus, where to eat, what time for practice; they all are minor details.

There were many more phrases but the one that has stuck with me all these years is, "Do the right thing." Football is a sport where there can be rule on top of rule for the collegiate athlete's behavior. Regardless of what other team's training rules were, the training rule for St. John's football players then was very simple, "Do the right thing."

When Bennies came visiting on campus in those days, one of the dorm rules was that all four feet had to be on the floor and the door had to be open as wide as a wastebasket. Now you could get pretty frisky and still be following those rules. However, then having five Johnnies peeping around the door yelling, "Did ya kiss her? Did ya kiss her?" would cool any romance. No rule is perfectly written, it's the intent and spirit of the rule application that matters.

That's not to say that some players didn't take advantage of the rule, it being conspicuously vague. At my one and only homecoming dance, I saw a table full of alcoholic beverages at a player's table that would have rivaled a bar. I couldn't believe it. A number of players were indulging in libations but the good players didn't push it. They knew the reality. Drinking would not help the team and it would not do them any good. So do the right thing, don't drink.

Those that did party too much and passed on good training habits would slowly fade from importance on the team. Their demise was from their lack of performance, not from John's scorn.

Doing the right thing has its own rewards. You may not become a better player. You will become a better person. It was amazing how, without being pushed by John, we worked ourselves hard to excel. It was not unusual to find players arriving early to practice working on fundamentals or running the stadium stairs after practice. All Johnnies have pushed themselves to win the national championship, it's the character of being a Johnnie. Few have had the honor of actually getting a national championship ring.

Drugs

Even in the remoteness of rural Stearns County and at St. John's campus in particular, in the late 1960s and early 1970s, there was no immunity from the evil of society—drugs.

In the peaceful halls of St. John's dormitories, one was never far from marijuana or other drugs. It wasn't published as to who had what, but one could always find drugs by asking around. The students didn't consider it a big deal then and I had the impression the faculty didn't either. St. John's was in an innocent state of mind. There was the unwritten code of "Don't ask, don't tell." I suspect that there were some punishments given out, but I was not aware of them and they were likely few and far between.

For myself, I admit, I had tried it and I had inhaled. It was soon apparent to me that I had a low tolerance for mind-altering substances. Whatever fun I might have had while high I never remembered afterwards. I decided early on that it wasn't for me that there was more to life than being high. My Johnnie experience with illegal drugs was minimal.

With my frequent trips to the hospital for football related injuries, it was routine for some dormitory mates to gleefully await my return with various potted plants collected. Within a day the flowers were gone and the soil cultivated with marijuana seeds. In time a dark green plant would emerge. With careful cultivation it would become a small, handsome looking bush. The colored foil wrapped base with ribbon and bow threw off everyone who looked at the plant. No one ever saw the tree from the forest. There were drugs in the open and no one knew it.

My drug experience during football occurred one year when I had a persistent cold and my sinuses had been stuffed up for days. It would not go away so I decided to try an over-the-counter cold remedy. The bottle stated something like one pill every two hours for four hours only. Well, by using new math, since I was twice as big as an average person I would adjust the dosage. Two for me would be the same as one for others and since the game would take more than two hours, might as well double the dose again. Hey, why not throw in a one more to knock the bug dead. By the time warm-ups were over, I was breathing fire and wound up tighter then the cables in the bell tower.

There was an upper classman on the team who didn't play much but filled the role of team motivator, always yelling "Get mean!" "Fire up!" "Let's go!" He especially liked to intimidate the underclassmen, getting in their faces and yelling. There was a drill we did just before taking the field to get ready for contact where we paired up, grabbed the same arm of a partner and slammed shoulder pads together. He grabs me and yells at me to fire up. In my stupor I grab his arm and started smashing him relentlessly with my shoulder. By the time we switched to our other arms he was quietly saying, "I think you're ready! That's enough! Ok! Ok!" I had knocked the stuffing out of him.

I thought I had played a terrific game but the Monday night film session proved otherwise. I took a lot of John's wrath that evening, lots of missed assignments and poor play. The next week I was still suffering from the cold and contemplated taking the medicine again as I was dressing for the game in the locker room. I knew it would make me feel like I was playing great and the stupor was intense, but I decided not to. I walked over and dropped the rest of the bottle into the trash and played in misery. The following Monday night film session went much better, no mistakes and better play.

My last experience with drugs was a classic St. John's melodrama. In my travels I had found an interesting substance to play with, cornstarch and water mixed into a thick, heavy paste. Squeeze it in your hand and it becomes solid like chalk, release the pressure and it slowly flows between your fingers like honey. Most bizarre. I bought a couple of boxes of cornstarch, filled forty or so small plastic baggies and put them into a shoebox. I had planned to sell them on campus to make a few bucks after Christmas break. When I returned I found the box missing and a note for my roommate and me to report to the Dean.

When we got there, on his desk was the shoebox with the baggies of cornstarch. Apparently, and I was not aware of this, during school breaks the dorm rooms are routinely searched for contraband. When they saw the cornstarch they though it was heroin. The first statement from the Dean was "Do you know that corn starch is used to cut heroin!" He said it like he had just recently learned that for himself. The suspicious bags were tested by state authorities and were found to be just pure cornstarch. The Dean noted that if the baggies had been heroin, that there was enough in the box to float Stearns County down the Mississippi River, an interesting concept.

I offered to demonstrate how the product worked but we were quickly shown the door.

Religion

     It's a no-brainer. A student at a religious university should know that they would eventually be required to take a religion course at some point in their schooling in order to graduate. But that didn't get me and quite a few other Johnnies to take such a class until our senior year. By then a student had to humbly go to the campus chaplain, Fr. Don, and ask for help in getting in the requirement or go to class with lowly freshman.

     When I showed up for Fr. Don's first class, I joined a large group of procrastinators. In the 1950s and 1960s, if you went to a Catholic grade school, your religion class experience was pretty much just memorizing of the Baltimore Catechism. You dreaded the thought of more of the same. We were in for a pleasant surprise. Fr. Don's class was one where there were no right and wrong answers, no classrooms to go to, just read the books, have informal discussions and write a paper or two. I can not say that I had any earth shaking revelations, but that wasn't the point. We were there to find our own religious path, whatever that may be.

     As a freshman from a devout Catholic family, the first Sunday on campus found me in church. By the second Sunday I realized that if I didn't go to church my parents would never know. By the third week on campus I had decided not to go to Sunday mass and I lived to talk about it. Not going to mass became easy and guilt was soon out the door.

Eventually some of the mass skippers got interested in going back, be it a campus ministry's mass with the Bennies or just something to do. For me, it was the position of my dorm room on 4th Benet, directly across from the church bell tower that boomed me out of bed every Sunday morning. Since I was up I would walk over to the church, go to mass and then go eat breakfast. Soon there was a group of us meeting at mass and going to breakfast afterwards. We didn't talk religion but we were being reverent by our association. Sometimes we would walk to the chapel across the lake and back to let the after-mass breakfast rush die down. It's just that type of community building and value determining that develops a religious conviction.

It wasn't a "born again" experience, the going back to mass, although I would say it was uplifting. In college you shed the forced rituals you grew up with and you develop a new view of what is best for you. That ranges from never going back to church again to going back to the same routines you had as a child, but with a new perspective.

I found church a good place to daydream, an escape from the day to day. A quiet, thoughtful time for contemplation and meditation. I cannot say that it was prayer in the usual sense, but whatever I was doing, it was good for me. In time as one gets older and life's problems pile up, the structure of religion offers more and more solace. We generally have whatever religion we were born into so the organization isn't as important as having faith.

The golden rule of all religions is to treat others as you would want to be treated yourself. We all search for our own understanding of that rule. A friend told me that he always acts in a manner such that if he were called into court to explain his actions, he could tell the truth and he would have nothing to hide. That puts a secular viewpoint on religion. If you expect to be held accountable for your deeds you will act accordingly.

In Europe there are many signs that read "CCTV" at business establishments. That stands for 'close circuit television' surveillance being on the premise and all activity is being recorded. In a religious perspective, that is a harsh view, that some fellow mortal is watching your every move so you better do the right thing. But it works to keep you on the straight and narrow, for there will be immediate consequences if you slip up.

      The best guidance is to know that there is a God who is watching over you. So be good, do the correct thing, even if only God knows. Besides, in today's world, who knows who else may be watching?

War

     I never was in the military and that is one aspect of my life that I have come to regret. My father served in the South Pacific in WWII and both my grandfathers were in Europe in WWI. About every man I knew while I was growing up had served in the military. Boys playing in the 1950s meant playing soldier, fighting the Germans and Japanese. I was a mute sentinel at my father's side, listening to him and other visitors to our home talk about their military experiences. I assumed I would go to war at some point in time since it seemed to be the inevitable destiny of all men.

     Through most of high school in the 1960s, I was oblivious to the Vietnam War. I had no idea what it was about other than something to watch on the evening news. I was in a daze. Towards the end of high school, an older kid in town was killed in Vietnam and he was brought home to be buried. Then I started to hear the protest songs and then they began to make sense. I still considered future military service to be a foregone conclusion, but now it was a somber business. Death was real and I didn't want to die.

     On a humid fall night my freshman year on 4th Benet in the fall of 1969, the hall fell quiet as the school radio station broadcast the first military draft since WWII. As dates were called off for the early draft numbers, muffled screams, curses and crashes of thrown objects, occasionally broke the silence. As more and more dates were called the noise level on the floor returned to normal and then everyone just forgot about it. I kept listening and finally at 300 or so my birthday was called. I didn't know then how significant that was, because in a few months my student deferment would be lost to poor grades. I would have been drafted had it not been for my high draft number.

There wasn't much selection on television behind the Pine Curtain when I was a student, just grainy black and white flickering reception. The television in the floor lounge would groan on late into the night, many times with old war movies. Some saw it as reality and some others saw it with cynicism.

A fellow freshman decided to enlist at Christmas our freshman year. I asked him why and he replied, "It's my duty." I also felt that calling, not to defend the country from some evil, but as a citizen it's what we were supposed to do.

I had scouted out the St. Cloud military service enlistment office, walking by numerous times, but I did not have the courage to walk in. I was formulating a game plan, my educational experience that fall semester 1969 at St. John's was not going well, my grades were poor and it appeared time to follow destiny's call.

My family let me take a car up to St. John's for the week of school before Christmas break. I used the occasion to go on my first collegiate date, with a nursing student from St. Cloud. We went to a movie, had a pizza and drove back to her dorm. Then a miraculous thing happened. This was the first date ever where I actually got kissed good-by and did not have a screen door slammed across my face or my date running off hysterically.

Suddenly there was a whole new game plan formulated; this dating thing was good. Hitchhiking to St. Cloud for a kiss was very doable and for the next two years it stayed very doable. When she graduated in the spring of 1972 our romance had died and I started to think again about military service. With one year to go it made sense to complete college and then enlist. I was well aware then that returning soldiers didn't adjust well to civilian life. It would be tough to go back to college after being in war. Since the Vietnam War seemed to be never ending, I would just wait until graduation before enlisting.

In the fourth quarter of a college basketball game in 1973, somewhere in Wisconsin, the public address speaker stopped the game and announced, "The war in Vietnam is over. A peace agreement has been signed!" As everyone stood up cheering, it hit me. Just like that my military service destiny was gone. No war, no need to serve. But wasn't I supposed to be in a war, any war, just like everyone before me? Guess not. Looking back at it, it may have been just a simple kiss that changed my fate and may well have kept me alive.

Great Plays

In the early 1960s the kitchen radio was the focus of attention in our home. Kids tuning in rock and roll while parents were switching back to talk radio. Many an early snowy morning was spent around the radio waiting to hear if our school was closing. Now I'm not talking about gathering around like the depression days of the 1930s. The television was the up and coming entertainment, but until we had a color television, radio was king.

With that in mind the greatest play I ever saw was on the radio. It was the first St. John's game in 1969, my freshman year, and we were playing an away game. The reason I didn't see it in person was that I didn't make the traveling team. I listened to the game on the campus radio station in my dorm room with the rest of the school. Dave, also a freshman, caught a long pass and ran for a touchdown. Maybe it was because he was one of us lowly freshman or maybe because of the way the radio announcer called it, "He's at the thirty! The twenty! The ten! Touchdown!" Regardless, being used to listening and imagining the action without seeing it made for a great play.

Bill was pound for pound one of the most exciting running backs I ever saw at St. John's. He was short and thin as a rail. He looked small on the field but could he run! He had two speeds, fast and faster. Sheer determination made him an outstanding player. On one play he was tackled at the line of scrimmage and he carried a number of defensive linemen for ten yards before they got him down. All you could see were two skinny legs running under a pile of opposing jerseys.

Jim made the greatest tackle I ever saw. My first year, we had lockers close together. As most freshman, I was more adolescent than adult. I had not yet physically matured as an athlete. Jim looked and played like a professional, big and powerful. He scared me, but a nicer person you would never meet. On one sweep towards his side, a burly pulling guard came running at him ready to bust a big gain. Jim was defending his defensive end position without support. As the guard lowered his shoulder, Jim crouched down and the blocker went airborne, flying over Jim. Jim then fired out and tackled the ball carrier. He hit him square with his shoulder pad, wrapped his arms, lifted the ball carrier up, drove him backwards and dropped him on his backside for a loss. It was picture perfect.

Then there was the game where my two roommates scored on St. Thomas. Early in a closely contested game, St. Thomas had the lead and was punting from deep in their own territory. Tom, a defensive end, told Steve, a defensive halfback, that he was going to hit the lineman opposite him to the outside so that Steve could cut inside and block the punt. It worked. Steve blocked the punt and Tom followed, scooping up the loose ball and ran it in for a touchdown. Just like clockwork.

Rick was a quarterback that hadn't made it at that position so he was switched to defensive back. He was putting a lot of time in on the bench when one of the starting defensive backs got hurt. The injured player was tall and was a well known defender. In an attempt to fool the opponents, John had Rick put on the hurt player's jersey and line up in his usual position. Since Rick was about six inches shorter than the injured player, when the jersey was tucked in, the bottoms of the numbers were at his belt. He looked like a junior high school player.

The question was would the opponents figure it out. On the first offensive play of the game, the opponents threw a pass right to Rick's side of the field. They knew. Rick gracefully stepped up into the path of the pass, cutting off the receiver and intercepted the ball. He was heartily congratulated on the sidelines when he came off the field and he quickly took off the large jersey, putting on his own, smaller one.

John did not believe in luck. It was hard work and preparation that made games go your way. Luck is the attitude of waiting until something happens in your favor without your participation. When you prepare and work hard, you make things go your way. But that's not to say that a favorable bounce of the ball or a beneficial call can't give you a welcomed advantage.

Even when we were being beaten, we would keep playing hard, playing our game and hoping for the best. That's the mentality of "expecting a miracle." Never give up because there is always the possibility that something will happen and then your hard work will have paid off. It doesn't always happen, but it can. Most people are defeated because they give up, not because they were beat. Play hard and by the rules and expect a miracle so that if one happens, you have positioned yourself to take advantage of it.

I learned from football that ordinary people could achieve extraordinary results. You just have to believe in yourself, work hard and be ready for an opportunity.

Farewell

One problem with life is that death follows. The longer we live the closer death is. A number of my college friends have passed away, mostly few and far between, but each one took a piece of me with them.

I saw an article in the newspaper about a woman who had died in an automobile accident in St. Paul. The name looked familiar, yet I could not place it. I passed on reading the whole article, however within a day there was another article on the same accident, so I read it through.

With each line I recognized familiar particulars about this person; a graduate from St. Benedict's, class of 1973, on various boards and volunteer groups, condolences from a past student I knew and the description of a well respected person. Then a sinking horror came over me and tears came down my cheeks. They listed the name of the person as Ann, but whom they were really writing about was the great Annie. I read the article a number of times through, hoping with each new reading that I might find something to indicate it wasn't Annie. But it was to no avail.

Annie was a person above reproach who served God and humanity with dignity and respect. Never the less, being human as we all are, she made a mistake and she paid for it with her life.

In the fall of 1969 St. Benedict's and St. John's were just starting to combine classes and having more social interaction. Most Johnnies did not have a clue as to what was happening around them so it was good to have that social contact. The women of St. Benedict's are good people and their descent on St. John's has had a profound effect.

The Bennies seemed to always be promoting some activity or cause on the Johnnies. One name that became synonymous with getting involved was that of Annie. More than once I would see someone trudging off to some activity and they would mutter that "Annie got me." The schools were small enough that the students knew who the movers and shakers were. I knew Annie was out to make the world a better place and that she was looking to get anyone and everyone involved. I tended to walk the other direction when I saw her because I knew she would try to get me embroiled in something.

I was awkward around women and I never seemed to connect with the Bennies. I just stayed with what I knew best, athletics. One fall I had been injured in a football game and was in the hospital. The first thing I saw when I woke up was a plate of chocolate chip cookies on the table next to the bed with a note on it wishing me well. It was signed by four or five Bennies, but the name that stuck out was Annie's. The unsinkable Annie had taken time for me.

When I made it back to school, I went to thank Annie. I told her it was the chocolate chip cookies that pulled me through. She was gracious to me and invited me to a party at St. Benedict's. Now I was finally ascending to the popular crowd on campus.

After a half-hour at that party, where I hadn't spoken a word to anyone, I got up to leave by excusing myself to no one in particular. As I walked out Annie came to me and thanked me for coming. Although she looked a bit put out that I would leave so early, it was my abysmal lack of social graces that had done me in. This just wasn't my type of fellowship. She politely acknowledged that and saw me to the door.

I would see Annie from time to time during our last years on campus and we would smile at each other, although I would avoid her whenever she was standing behind a table with papers on it. Over the years I would see her picture in the newspaper or read a story about her in the alumni magazine. I always appreciated her kindness and admired her strength and power. And I have always believed in the power of the chocolate chip cookie.

Discrimination

I grew up in a lily-white suburban neighborhood of St. Paul, Minnesota. There were no people of color in our town that I was aware of, none in the schools, stores or churches. In the late 1950s, about the only people of color I saw were train porters and elevator operators when my family went on trips and to doctor appointments in St. Paul.

The only discrimination I had in my early years was against, of all people, Germans. As was the common practice for boys in those days, playtime usually involved playing war and the enemies of choice were German and Japanese soldiers. The end of World War II was only ten or so years previous. Just about all our fathers had fought in the war and they were still talking about it as they dealt with their readjustment issues.

As it happened, there was a recently immigrated family from Germany in our town that had a boy my age and in my class. His name was Warner. He was a typical wild, loud and totally oblivious grade school child who also liked to play war. As to be expected, his just being German and his ability to speak German put him in the cross hairs of our make believe guns and grenades. From an adult's point of view, it was darn right cruel. But to a kid in grade school, it was viewed as fun. In time, however, it wore on Warner. A macho solider can only take on the world for so long before it gets tiring and lonely.

At an evening school function where our parents were present for a pot luck meal, my classmates and I were playing war, running up and down to school halls by the cafeteria where the parents were. Either we were chasing Warner or he was chasing us and we all ended up in a classroom, shooting at each other from behind the desks.

Suddenly someone yelled out "Run. Warner's dad is coming!" With that we all, Warner included, jumped into the coat lockers in the back of the room and waited to see if we were going to get caught.

We watched through the cracks in the doors as the light was turned on and as Warner's dad walked into the classroom. "Boys," he said, "come out of the lockers." Out we humbly walked; young children are not terribly adept when it comes to avoiding the consequences of their acts.

As would any father, Warner's dad asked why we gave Warner such a hard time. Of course he knew why, it was because of his Germanic heritage. Then Warner's dad did an amazing thing. He started telling stories about his experiences in the war as a German solider.

We were riveted. He could not tell enough stories. Eventually we were relaxed enough to ask him questions. I asked him if he ever retreated from a battle.

"Yes. When I was on the Russian front, I ran for weeks to get back to Germany." Well he was short and stocky and had no appearance of being an athlete. I questioned him on how he could run for days on end.

"If you want to live, you can do amazing things." He said. "I didn't sprint but I jogged for long periods of time, rested and then started jogging again, day and night. If the Russians had caught me, they would have killed me."

We still played war after that and Warner was still the object of most attacks. I came to believe he actually enjoyed it as long as the rest of us would talk to him afterwards and treated him as an equal. The ironic part is that I later found out that my own ancestry was half German.

St. John's did have students of color but many of them were from the Benedictine mission schools from other countries. On my freshman dorm floor there was a fellow of Hispanic descent who came from the Caribbean. I assumed he was just like the Hispanics I saw in the movie, *West Side Story*—a ladies' man who carried a knife. He was very charming with the ladies, but he also helped us less tactful gents to meet women. He had no chip on his shoulder; he was a good person.

Another fellow on my floor was a black man from the Bahamas. He spoke with a British accent and was very proper in all mannerism. On a floor outing the first week at school, he wore an impeccable white suit of clothes that one might see at a cricket match. Not what I was expecting after watching all the race riots on television in the late 1960s.

There were American people of color at St. John's, but I did not have contact with them in my everyday campus activities so I had little if any interaction with them.

My awakening lesson in race relations came on a road trip to Florida on Easter Break my freshman year. We had been driving for 20 plus hours and we were stopped at a gas station in southern Georgia around 7:00 AM. Half asleep, I grabbed and pulled the restroom handle to enter, but someone on the inside also had their hand on it. It did not open, so thinking it was stuck, I pulled harder and the door popped open. Suddenly I was confronted by a short, well dressed black man who immediately jumped to the side. He would not make eye contact, looked down at his feet and said in a very articulate voice "I am sorry sir. This will never happen again!"

This was my first contact, one on one, with a person of color and I was shaking in fear. I was so scared I could not walk; I had to wait until the fellow left. Again he stated profusely while deliberately looking down and refusing to make eye contact, that he was sorry and that it would not happen again. Even though I had a foot in height and 100 pounds of weight on him I was too scared to move.

I have found that the best way to stop prejudice is to grab the feeling tight and hold it so it is never known to others. Never let biased thoughts out; never lose control and express them. Eventually they will die out and you will be free.

As Only Freshman Are

My first year at St. John's found me a naive, unworldly and unsophisticated person. I ended up in a dorm of similarly natured persons, the 4th floor of Benet Hall. That fact was likely not lost on the senior who wandered all the way up there to see if anyone would volunteer to put on a comedy sketch for homecoming festivities.

He asked for us to write up and put on some kind of comedy play for the homecoming rally in the gym. The directions given were that it should be some type of parody on sports with the upcoming homecoming opponent being the villain or victim of the performance. We agreed and as he left he turned around and quietly mentioned that since it was just St. John's students who would be viewing it, we should try to make it repulsive and vulgar so the crowd would get into it and be riled up.

As it happened there was a budding comic genius on the floor who quickly wrote up a repugnant enough skit. I was picked to be the hero, or heroine in this case, Polly Purebreast, a female wrestler in St. John's colors. To counter my 6' 5" and 225 pound size my opponent was a 5' 6' and 120 pound fellow student, given the name Snake, who wore the homecoming opponent's colors. There was no doubt about what the essence and outcome of the wrestling match was to be.

The referee was Wally Carballs and the innuendo went downhill from there. My feminine endowment was enhanced by a couple of strategically placed volleyballs. The calls of the referee during the match were to be laced with double meanings and suggestive phrases that would have disgusted even the manliest of men.

On the day of the performance we gathered just outside the gym doors and waiting for our cue. I had taken off my glasses so I did not notice that the crowd included not only rabid Johnny students, but their dates and various faculty members, including the Dean. The fellow playing Snake had second thoughts and suggested we not go through with it, but he was quickly overruled.

As we walked out the obvious nature and direction of the skit got the Johnnies fired up into a fevered pitch. With the start of the wrestling portion Snake got stage fright and froze up; he would not go through the scripted stances. Yes, our match was staged!

I ended up having to grab him and manhandle him into the various positions. For the finale, I used the "secret move," a quick pop to the head with one of my discretely placed volleyballs. Since Snake was having no part in the choreographed fighting, I had to chase him down and I just about knocked him out to finish the skit.

We assumed everything went well, the crowd cheered wildly and the homecoming program was a success. The first notice of something running afoul was when a senior football player told me that the play was disgusting, that he was embarrassed for his date that he had taken to the performance and he wanted to punch me out. I left quickly.

On the following Monday morning, all the participants received word from the floor prefect that we were to go down to see the Dean. The shine was definitely off the performance. We trudged into the Dean's office and sitting there, with the Dean, who was at the performance, was the senior who had put us up to it. The senior quickly washed his hands of us, stating that he only asked for a humorous play and that he had nothing to do with the raunchiness.

As freshmen, all we could do was point to the senior and say, "Ya, but...." It was to no avail. I suspect our innocence of being hoodwinked into doing the skit was evident enough to the Dean, he let us go with a warning. We were on pins and needles for the rest of the fall semester not wanting to get called into the Dean's office again.

    The lesson learned was to not be so gullible. We knew that what we were doing was in poor taste and that we should have thought it through more thoroughly.

Money

Comparing the monetary cost of goods and services between the 1960s/1970s and today is a study in absurdity. Tuition my first year at St. John's was $1,600.00, room was $200.00 and board was another $200.00. That was for the whole year. Gasoline was $0.29 a gallon for all the years I was there until the first oil embargo in the spring of 1973. That being said, however, the principles of money management have not changed over time.

The tenant of "only spend the money you have" applied then as it applies today. In the past, one could get into financial problems. But today it can be done easier and quicker. Credit cards for students were unheard of in my college days. Very few students even had checking accounts. Other than saving accounts, financial transactions for college students then were pretty much limited to cash on the barrelhead.

Life was simpler then, few cars and no cell phones. The dorms had one hall telephone per floor. There was no privacy in the hall so most telephone calls were made at pay phones in phone booths, the good old "pay as you go" system where you first put in a coin and then you used the telephone.

St. John's was isolated so entertainment came to campus. The dances and movies on campus were subsidized by the school so costs were minimal. About the only place to spend discretionary money on campus was at the student union.

I did not earn much money the summer before my freshman year so I lived that year on the cheap. Other than birthday cash and Christmas loot, I was always out of money. Most of the cash I did have I spent on washing clothes. I helped out at the campus movie theater so I was able to see the movies for free. Dances were few and far between and since I was worthless with women, dances were not a financial burden.

Some students had a lot of money and it was tough to walk through the student union and see them playing foosball, pool and buying snacks. Many a time I would stare at a candy bars under the glass counter top with my hand squeezing hard on the change in my pocket. The perceived pleasure of eating the candy was countered by the pain of squeezing the coins harder and harder. Usually, I would decide to save my money and walk away with a redden hand from grasping the change so firmly.

I had good paying summer jobs the rest of my summers between school years at St. John's. I was able to help pay my parents back for some of the schooling costs and I put away about $2.00 a week for spending money during the school year. Tax refund time was highly anticipated.

Another tenant of money management was quickly learned. "No matter how much money you have, you never have enough." Although my finances were greatly improved after my first year, I would still find myself short of money by the weekend. Luckily I was disciplined enough go without, to not spend more than what I had allotted myself for each week.

There were some jobs available on campus to earn money. Most were worked into financial aid packages, but the really desperate found work shoveling coal at the power plant. Some students would find themselves dead broke and believing that they could not exist without money or found themselves owing money to anxious fellow students.

St. John's was self sufficient for many years. Coal was brought in by railroad cars for electrical generation and heat production and had to be shoveled around at the power plant. It was bad enough that it was a dirty job, but the shoveling was done at night. Some mornings, as I would be heading out to an early class, I would see a fellow student slowly walking back to the dorm in coveralls, filthy with coal dust. The students did not stay at that job more than a few days; some life lessons are learned quickly.

By my fifth year I had purchased a car and assumed the associated costs. My parents covered the insurance, but gas and maintenance were on my dime. I was able to stay on top of all the various expenses until graduation.

Suddenly I found myself broke and in need of money. I had no intention of shoveling coal so I decided to cash in my graduation cap and gown fee. It was a December graduation so the pomp and ceremony would be minimal. I went to the Bursar's Office and received a refund of the $10.00 or so fee and although gasoline had jumped to around 70 cents per gallon, I was able to buy enough gas to get home.

A Life Less Frantic

One never knows how valuable or good something is until it is gone. I am like many Baby Boomers who are edging into their elderly years of life with children grown, careers winding up and spending more time reminiscing about the past. The computer information explosion and the desire to be interconnected to the world make our lives a constant whirl of activity. As we work harder and harder at living, we have less and less time for boredom.

Yes boredom, those moments in time when we sits and thinks or sometimes we just sits. Before life got so demanding we thought of boredom as a waste of time. Now we should see it as those precious moments of time where we can collect our thoughts and refresh our mind, a time to slow down the constant bombardment of stimuli to the brain.

St. John's, as were many college campuses in the 1970s, was a good place to perfect the art of boredom. Of course you had to first accept boredom as something less than a waste of time. Some people never did handle boredom well so they strove to keep busy all the time. The isolation and space provided by St. John's allowed for great moments in boredom, or more specifically, thinking without direct purpose.

When you sit at a desk and work on homework or a class reading assignment, you are thinking with a purpose—learning. When you are sitting on an outside bench on a warm spring day staring out at nothing in particular, you are thinking without purpose—daydreaming. Daydreaming is a great human creative thought process. It ties random ideas together, even if nothing comes from it right away. The association is left recessed in the brain to possibly be used another day or to maybe never be used again.

Boredom can also produce the feelings of sadness and social anxiety. Everyone carries a degree of depression in themselves and everyone has to deal with it in his or her own way. Most are able to take the ebb and flow of emotions in stride, but some need help.

At St. John's, I learned to ride the roller coaster of emotions. They would take me from highs to lows and back again. The trick was to be patient with the lows and in time a high would come. Being afraid that the low would persist made it persist.

I had (and have) no problem with asking God for help. Mostly there never was an immediate answer but by just asking, at the very least, I was no longer fixated on an issue. I would use a short phrase like "Lord Jesus, have mercy on me, I am a sinner" and repeat it a many times. Repeating that with rhythmic, deep, long breaths also helps in falling asleep!

The best relief is human contact. Friends are best if you can find one to talk to. At St. John's I generally made contact with a stranger. If there is an exchange of words, no matter how trivial, then there is a person to person contact and an acknowledgement of existence. By reaching out to another, you shared a human encounter with another human being, who no doubt, has his or her own issues. You both gain.

The significance of a liberal art education is having been taught how to think. The hustle and bustle of today's world makes finding time to think harder to do. Too much of our existence is spent taking in data, processing it and moving on to more data. That leaves little time to think through what we have taken in.

That's why good old fashion boredom is needed today. To think through and connect the information we have received from our day to day existence. Give yourself respite from the mental fatigue of staying on task. Take off the headphones and listen to silence. Stare out and daydream and do not worry about wasting time or being different, life carries on.

A Great Game

    Every athlete has his or her greatest sport's moment. For me, it was the 1971 football game when St. John's played host to St. Cloud State (now called St. Cloud State University) at Collegeville.

    The set up for the game started a year earlier in the late summer of 1970. St. John's had a good year in 1969, winning the Mineral Water Bowl and posting an 8-1-1 record. The prognosticators at the Sports Illustrated magazine had it that St. John's would be the top Division III team in 1970 so St. John's got the number one ranking in their pre-season poll.

    It was an honor to be recognized as the top team, but it also brought with it a curse. There was a target on our backs and everyone was aiming for it. Before the season started, the ranking was the butt of a lot of joking. "Is that the number '51' or the letters 'SI' (for Sports Illustrated) on the back of your jersey?"

    The season started well with a convincing 38 to 0 victory over Wartburg of Iowa. That was the only overnight travel game I was on at St. John's. We slept two to a bed except for the few married fellows, they slept alone. No one would share a bed with them. The next game was against cross town rival St. Cloud State.

    St. Cloud is a Division II team; they can have football scholarships and conduct spring football practice whereas Division III teams can not. That plus the proximity of the schools made for an intense rivalry. The bull's-eye on our backs was shining bright that afternoon as St. John's lost 34 to 22 in front of a large crowd at St. Cloud's old Selke Field. After the game, the St. Cloud players ran by the Johnnie bench, holding up their index finger and shouting, "We're number one!" It was a bit over the top but not to worry, next year we will play them at home. That 1970 season was not filled with glory. We went 6-3. Were we victims of the curse of publicity?

The 1971 season began without any pre-season hype. We again started with a strong 49-13 victory over Wartburg. Next it was St. Cloud for some unfinished business.

In those days, we dressed in the old "Rat Hall" gymnasium locker rooms, waked across the campus and down the storied south stairs onto the field, in a never ending procession of red jerseys (100 plus dressed players for home games). There was the feeling of empowerment from history that engulfed you when entering the football stadium in those days. Three undefeated teams and two national championship teams had walked those very steps in the last 10 years. You felt the power and the history.

It was one of the quietest walks ever. I had visions of St. Cloud players running around and shouting "We're number one" dancing in my head. Gagliardi didn't say much as we did our pre-game warm up. No need to.

Although we had great passers and receivers then, football in the early 1970s relied more on the running game. The drives could take five to seven minutes to go down the field, grinding out five yard gains over and over. Today the passing game is much stronger and scoring drives can take just a few minutes.

That year I was the weak-side tackle on the offensive line. The offensive end on my side was split out so I was the last inside man on the line of scrimmage. Key plays that came to my side were either sweeps where I would hook the person positioned over me and the ball carrier would run to the outside, or traps where I would block down and the person over me would get blocked out by a pulling guard with the ball carrier running inside.

I was having my way with the defender over me. If he played me straight up I would run past him. When he cheated outside I would hook him. When he got farther outside we trapped him. Eventually he was played way off the line of scrimmage and getting beat regularly. As my game was going, so was the team's. We scored just about every time we had possession of the ball with long drives up and down the field.

At the end of the third quarter the score was St. John's 32, St. Cloud 0. The score does not really tell the story of the game up to that point. Our defense had held them to minimal offensive yardage. Basically, St. John's had thoroughly and methodically had crushed St. Cloud. They could not stop us, it was a thumping.

The final score was 32-7, but by the 4th quarter the game was over. St. Cloud was not able to mount any significant offense. After I was pulled late in the game, I sat on the bench in the hot sun with a smile on my face. Job well done.

That 1971 season saw St. John's develop into an unexpectedly strong team. We went 8-1 with the only loss being at Duluth, another Division II team. That was the infamous 22-21 loss where we had a 21-16 lead with minutes left in the game and the ball close to the Duluth goal line.

Do we kick a field goal and give Duluth a kickoff with the chance to get the ball in scoring position from the kickoff, possibly score a touchdown and go for two points to tie the game? Or do we go for a touchdown to ice the game, but take the unlikely chance that if we do not score that Duluth could drive the length of the field to score a touchdown for the win, with just a couple of minutes left in the game? We went for the touchdown.

Those last few minutes of the game have become the spawn of many nightmares. With apologies to Ernest Thayer and his poem *Casey at the Bat*:
> "Oh, somewhere in this favored land the sun is shining bright;
> The band is playing somewhere, and somewhere hearts are light,
> And somewhere men are laughing, and somewhere children shout;
> But there is no joy in Collegeville—mighty St. John's has lost."

Values

I do not believe life was better in the good old days then it is today. Modern times have brought many wonderful and amazing advances in communication, medicine and in life generally. There are, however, some facets of yesterday that are still universal truths today that have been diminished in today's world.

One is the axiom that "life is not fair, live with it." When I was in grade school, if one of the nuns hit me, whether it was justified or not, I would never have told my parents. They would have, and I would have expected them to—hit me again. A lot of what life deals out is not fair, but I believe it is evened out over time. The trick is to have patience and wait for the next hand dealt, that one may be better.

At St. John's, the stoic German attitude did not allow for grousing when you came up short. If the good desserts were all gone when you went through the food line, you didn't ask the server for more, you went without. You made a mental note to get there earlier next time and accepted fate as it happened. By not making a scene and demanding equal results, one grows a bit stronger and tougher. You need to make the best of what you have been given.

When everyone accepts the ideal that life is not fair and lives with it, it becomes easier to get along with others. If I got something I wanted and I know someone else who wanted it didn't get it, and if we both understand that the next time the situation could be reversed, we both have less envy with each other.

The opposite of the "life is not fair, live with it" lesson is "entitlement." Entitlement is the curse of a society bent on the philosophy of "Me. Me. Me." If so and so got such and such, why didn't I?

People have learned that complaining, playing the "bad service" card and just making a scene can and does work. It's not the job of the service and product providers to equalize all things to all people; rather, everybody has to realize that life does not always work out the way you had hoped. So accept what you have and do it with an understanding heart.

There is power to be had from the times where one did not get a good shake of the dice yet accepted the results. The yearning to possess that which someone else has received will only eat your soul out. What you get is what you need.

Working hard can provide for more, but seeing hard work only as a certainty for getting more is wrong. One will never get everything one wants if it is measured by envy for what others have. Get everything we want leads us to perdition, slow and sure.

St. John's had a great example of accepting life as it is and avoiding entitlement by the life examples lived by the Benedictines on campus. That exemplar was all around the campus but you had to look or you would not see it. It's not just the Benedictine's vow of poverty; rather, it was the application of the Rule of St. Benedict to live a good life with the well being of others being the guide.

We do not live in a perfect world, yet it is good enough. By having reasonable expectations, happiness is more readily attainable.

Classic Moments

St. John's has an old theater that was used for movies almost every weekend when I was a student there. The movies were generally newer or unique releases; at least I never saw them elsewhere before they were shown on campus. The weekly movie was generally the highlight of most weekends, especially when the cold winter winds were blowing. They were well attended.

One movie that was featured was *The Boys in the Band*. It is a story about the coming to terms of the main character's sexual orientation within the context of a male musician's group that included some homosexual persons. I was unaware of the nature of the film because I had not taken the time to read the monthly movie flyer, as I suspect many others in the audience had also not read.

Once the plot of the film was revealed, there was a tense atmosphere in the theater. The audience identified with the main character. Everyone questions their own sexuality and at an all men's institution, there is even more consternation. Everybody was intensely watching the film and one could have heard the preverbal pin drop.

There came a scene where the actors played a sort of spin-the-bottle game in which the party chosen had to call the one they loved. They could call whomever they wanted, but they had to make a call and reveal who it was. The characters called, one by one, girlfriends and boyfriends.

When the main character's turn came up, he made his call. The telephone rang many times, droning on in the theater. After a time the ringing stopped and there was a long moment of absolute silence on and off the screen.

Then in a voice mimicking the cadence of a 1940s movie dialog where a hotel bellhop walks through a crowded lobby and loudly calls out; a wit in the audience proclaimed, "Telephone call for B----- B-----."

The audience burst into laughter as BB was well known on campus and he was also in the theater. As people were falling off their seats from hysterics, BB found the wit and was summarily pounding him. Luckily some in the audience were able to hold BB back until he settled down. I do not remember what happened in that scene, but the air in the theater was more relaxed for the balance of the movie.

Well placed levity can help to alleviate the anxiety of tense subject matter, which is what generally helps in stressful situations.

* * * *

Each player on a football offense team has an assignment for every play. If everybody is successful in their assignment on a play, in theory, the offensive team should score a touchdown.

Late in one game when the reserve players were being substituted in, the St. John's quarterback called an inside double-reverse play. That is a slow developing play where the quarterback goes right and hands off the ball to the halfback who goes left and he makes a second hand off to the third running back who goes back right again and turns up the field just over the center to gain yardage. If all the assignments are carried out successfully it is a spectacular play that has the crowd and defense guessing where the ball is.

On one running of that play, the third running back gained about 20 yards. He was tackled by the last player between him and the goal line. A good play all and all.

As it happened with victories, John would be more critical of assignment errors at the Monday night film reviews then he was with losses. When that play was reviewed, John ran the film projector over and over, maybe 10 times. When John was quiet at those times you had to guess what he was looking at. It soon became evident that he was focusing in on just one player.

On the snap of the ball, the split end who was far away from the ball handling, took two quick steps, bobbed his head for a fake pass cut and pulled up to watch the play unfold. His assignment was to block the defensive player covering him. By not blocking his assigned player, that defensive player took off across the filed for the ball carrier and made the tackle that prevented a touchdown.

John never said a word. He just kept running the projector back and forth until everyone in the auditorium knew what the issue was, a blown assignment due to inattentiveness that prevented a perfect play and a touchdown. Everyone else had completed their assignment except the split end.

Now John was not averse to express his feelings on blown assignments and I had felt his wrath many times. That is a good thing; he is trying to help you. Not getting yelled at is a bad thing. That player slowly faded away, not earning a starting position while I was there.

Actions can speak louder than words.